BRIDGING THE PERFORMANCE GAP

Bridging the Performance Gap

Trevor J. Bentley

Gower

Published by
Gower Publishing Limited
Gower House
Croft Road
Aldershot
Hampshire GU11 3HR
England

Gower
Old Post Road
Brookfield
Vermont 05036
USA

British Library Cataloguing in Publication Data

Bentley, Trevor J.
    Bridging the performance gap
    1. Employee motivation   2. Performance   3. Employees – Rating of
    I. Title
    658.3'14

ISBN 0 566 07760 4

Library of Congress Cataloging-in-Publication Data

Bentley, Trevor J.
    Bridging the performance gap / by Trevor J. Bentley.
        p.   cm.
    ISBN 0–566–07760–4
    1. Employee motivation.   2. Performance.   I. Title.
    HF5549.5.M63B46   1996
    658.3'14—dc20   96–8725
                                                                        CIP

Typeset in Palatino and Helvetica by Bournemouth Colour Press and printed in Great Britain by Hartnolls Ltd, Bodmin.

Contents

Figures

Tables

Preface

Having worked in a variety of positions in and for organizations for forty years I have come to realize that the way people perform is conditioned more by the environment and the way they are treated than by the presence or lack of particular competencies. For the last fifteen years I have worked as a consultant – helping organizations, groups and individuals to improve their performance – and have found that people primarily focus on developing competencies.

This attention to developing competencies is based on the simple hypothesis that if you increase the level of competency then improved performance will follow. Unfortunately this rational and logical approach is only part of the answer.

The missing ingredient is neither rational nor logical, in fact it is the exact opposite. What converts competence into performance are the irrational and illogical ways that people choose to put their energy into some particular endeavour. It is these choices that people make that far outweigh the competency factor in the performance equation.

This book is about discovering and paying attention to these irrational and illogical aspects of human behaviour that have such an effect on performance. Its aim is to define the 'missing ingredient' and to establish simple and practical ways of bridging the performance gap.

My research for this book has been mainly based on my own experience working with organizations trying to bridge the performance gap. Whilst there is a considerable amount of literature on training, learning, appraisal, development, mentoring and coaching, and more recently competency development, there is a distinct lack of material on performance. Most of what is available seems to focus on the input to the performance process rather than the outcomes. The result of this 'input' focus is that performance becomes what we know we can do rather than the possibilities inherent in our potential.

I was walking in the Lake District with a group of friends when we came to a stream. The stream was in flood and the usual crossing place was a roaring torrent. We backtracked until we found a place where the stream appeared crossable. Several of the group took a short run and jumped the stream. An elderly, portly member of the group tried and fell full length into the stream. He was quickly dragged out and seemed none the worse for wear, except that he was wet.

'I knew I couldn't do it' he said with a grin, 'but I just thought, I'll have a go and see what happens, and here I am on the opposite side of the stream. I suppose I could've waded across, but trying to jump seemed more fun.'

If my friend's objective was to jump the stream then he failed. However his desired outcome was to cross the stream, which he succeeded in doing. The difference then between success and failure in this case was how the outcome was perceived.

If we always follow the rational and logical approach based on our known competencies with the assumption that with these competencies we can achieve X, then we will always achieve X and $X+$ will seem an impossible goal. Of course we need to have a certain level of competency to perform a particular task, i.e. to achieve X, and we need something else to achieve $X+$ and it isn't more competency.

The reasonable man adapts himself to the world: the unreasonable one persists in trying to adapt the world to himself. Therefore all progress depends on the unreasonable man.

Reason, George Bernard Shaw

Trevor J. Bentley

Acknowledgements

A book of this nature cannot be written without the input of other people either knowingly and willingly or by default through working with me. There are many people I need to thank from all the organizations I have worked with and they will know who they are. However, I would like to say thank you in particular to Howard Boorman, Scott Archibald, and Marty Klumpp for the work we did together in Westpac in Australia; to Alan Smith for my work with him and the team at the National Australia Group in Europe; to Warner Manning at HSBC, and Sue Clayton, Malcolm Parlett and all my friends on the Gestalt in Organisations Group; to my friends on the Performance Management Forum and last but not least to my wife Liz.

TJB

Part 1

The nature of performance

1   The performance gap

It is not the clay which makes a pot valuable
Nor is it the pot's shape
The pot's value
comes from the shape of the space the clay enfolds.

There is a paradox in this idea taken from Lao Tzu. The thought that a potter is the moulder of space rather than clay is both a contradiction of what we think we see the potter doing and what we perceive as the outcome of the potter's craft.

The same paradox and contradiction exists when we talk about performance. Is it what we see people doing that is performance, or is it the outcome of their efforts which is performance? If we believe that it is what we see people doing then we can measure performance by looking at how well they are doing what they are doing. This is a competency-based approach to measuring performance. On the other hand if we believe that performance is the outcome of what people do then we have to measure it by measuring outcomes, and the degree of competency displayed or not displayed is less important.

So here is the paradox – we need to be competent to perform, but competency does not of itself result in performance.

In order to decide what constitutes the performance gap it is necessary to examine what we mean by performance. There are three important elements of performance – expectations, outcomes and results.

Expectations are those things that we anticipate will or think should happen. These can be both realistic (those I think I can achieve) and unrealistic (those I think I cannot achieve). If I am a performer and I know what is *expected* of me this gives me an idea of how others will measure my performance, i.e. in terms of meeting, or failing to meet these *expectations*. If these expectations are well within my ability to achieve and I am sufficiently motivated to achieve them then I will appear to be a good performer. If they are unrealistic and outside what I believe I can achieve there is little I can do and I will probably be demotivated. Even if they are within my reach I may choose not to meet them.

Outcomes are the things produced by my efforts to meet the expectations. They are the *outputs* of my performance. If my main concern is performance then the exact way I manage to produce these outcomes is probably not important except as a part of my learning process.

Results are the impact that my *outcomes* have on the environment in which I am performing. They are what happens because of the *outcomes* I have produced.

I work as a consultant. In order to be able to measure my performance I need to know:

- what my customers expect from me
- the specific nature of the outcomes from my work
- the results these outcomes will have.

Here is an example of the performance indicators from a team development project:

Expectations

That I will work closely with the management team to assess and comment on the way the team works together and to suggest improved ways of working.

Outcomes

1 Improved communications leading to better working relationships, shorter management meetings and improved support for each other.
2 A willingness to take ownership of and responsibility for decisions.
3 A greater degree of sharing workloads and helping each other deal with difficulties.
4 An individual willingness to ask for help when needed.

Results

Improved morale.
Improved profits.

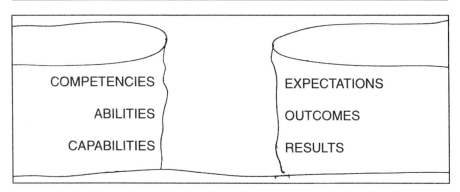

COMPETENCIES	EXPECTATIONS
ABILITIES	OUTCOMES
CAPABILITIES	RESULTS

Figure 1.1   The 'performance gap'

Improved (happier) working environment.
Reduced stress (more supportive environment).

You will notice that there is nothing in this statement of performance that is concerned with my competencies to meet these expectations and to produce the outcomes and achieve the results stated. The paradox is that it doesn't matter what my competencies are and how extensive my CV is, or how hard I work, if I don't meet these performance criteria *I have not performed.*

My competence, ability, and capability to perform is of no matter if I don't do what I agree I can do. Nor does any display of my apparent abilities mean anything if I don't perform.

So here is the 'performance gap' – between what I am apparently capable of and what I achieve in terms of meeting expectations, producing outcomes and achieving results (see Figure 1.1).

The critical factors

There are five critical factors that determine the extent of the performance gap, and which can affect anyone no matter how competent and capable they may be. They are:

- the environment
- the conditions
- personal desires
- personal state
- personal competence.

The environment

The environment in which we perform is very important in supporting, or not supporting our efforts. It can cover many aspects of the workplace – our colleagues, the facilities we have access to, the premises and so on. For example, in order to foster improved customer services many banks have redesigned the 'front office' to be a more welcoming and hospitable place. Attention to the environment in which people are going to perform is part of the process of bridging the performance gap.

The conditions

The conditions under which we perform can help or hinder depending on what is happening at any one point of time. If the conditions involve pressure because the office is short staffed performance will suffer. If the conditions demand attention to a particular code of behaviour and there are fixed rules and procedures to follow then again performance may be limited. (There are of course some situations where strict codes of practice are essential.) On the other hand if the prevailing conditions allow people to use initiative and explore their potential then performance will improve.

Personal desires

One aspect of performance that is often overlooked by management is the personal desire of the individual to perform. This can vary from day to day and has a significant effect on what people do. All kinds of approaches have been tried in the attempt to motivate people to work harder, or perform better. Often these have been under the banner of 'productivity improvement'. They range from incentive schemes and piece work to holidays abroad or use of the managing director's Rolls-Royce for a few weeks. Money, status, prizes, and recognition as 'employee of the month' have all been used as a means of promoting increased desire to perform, yet the underlying and critical factor is still whether people want to do it or not.

Personal state

If I am physically unwell and/or psychologically affected in some way I am not going to perform very well. How we feel varies all the time but we are expected to perform at the same high level regardless. This attitude of turning a blind eye to the current state people are in is in fact counter productive. By placing more pressure on people who are not in a fit state to deal with it actually worsens performance. Acknowledging that personal state can have an impact and adjusting expectations accordingly will, I believe, lead to less time off sick, less absenteeism, and overall improved performance.

Personal competence

Of course people do need to have the competence to perform at the expected levels. It is important to know what levels of competence are needed for what is expected. With this information it is possible to pay attention to enhancing competencies accordingly. However, simply improving competence does not necessarily lead to improved performance.

Identifying the missing ingredient

In any particular situation where performance is not reaching the expected levels there has to be some 'missing ingredient' to which sufficient attention is not being paid. Discovering the 'missing ingredient' means looking at the circumstances and examining the five critical factors. For each of the factors it is desirable to determine their effect on performance and how improvements can be made to support higher levels of performance (see Table 1.1).

Finding the 'missing ingredient' demands a very open and honest review of what is happening at the present time, and should involve the people managing performance and the performers themselves. It is usually true to say that the performers are the best source of information about what the missing ingredient is, unfortunately they are often not listened to attentively.

Table 1.1   Searching for the 'missing ingredient'

Critical factors	Current impact on performance	Possible improvements
The environment		
The conditions		
Personal desires		
Personal state		
Personal competence		

Management are often surprised to see how much time I spend observing and listening to the performers when I am carrying out a 'performance review'. By doing this it is usually possible to discover and define the 'missing ingredient'.

Measuring the 'performance gap'

Having discovered the 'missing ingredient' we should then measure the extent of the 'performance gap'. Imagine trying to build a bridge without knowing the gap that has to be spanned. The approach is depicted in terms of 'where we are' and 'where we want to be' (see Figure 1.2). In this exercise it is important to be able to have a vision about what high performance, or if you prefer, success will look like.

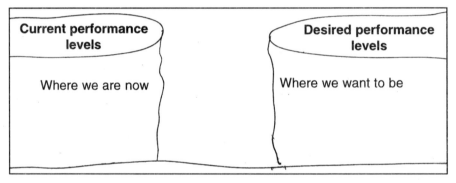

Figure 1.2   The extent of the 'performance gap'

'Where we are' is usually easy to assess, although there are situations where establishing performance indicators does present difficulties. It is important to focus on the three levels mentioned earlier, namely: expectations, outcomes and results. When this has been completed we can move on to the other side of the gap.

'Where we want to be' is less easy to assess because there is often a problem in distinguishing between what is possible and what is not. People and organizations should have a vision of how they want things to be and if the target is pushed too far out it becomes almost impossible to build a bridge. Perhaps what we need is a vision and then a closer view of the first gap we have to cross to get there. It is much better to set realistic aims and then to reassess performance later and build another bridge. So instead of one massive bridge we build a series of smaller ones.

In establishing both sides of the divide it is important to involve everyone concerned. Managers often argue that if people are left to set their own performance targets they will set ones which are easy to reach and there will be no 'stretch factor' in them. This is sometimes true, but it is also true that people often set themselves targets that management would not even dare suggest.

Building bridges

Building bridges is a team effort. The organization, management and the performers themselves are all involved in the process. For bridges to be built successfully everyone involved has to know exactly what their part is in the process. This means that we need blueprints, worksheets and stage posts.

Blueprints

Blueprints are the plans and detailed drawings of how the bridge will be constructed. They have to include specific details for each of the five critical performance factors that have been identified as the 'missing ingredients'. The more care taken in preparing the blueprints the more successful the bridge building will be.

Worksheets

Worksheets are needed for each person involved, including performers and managers. Each worksheet will set out what they have to do in the bridge building that is taking place. The worksheets set out the tasks and the timescales for completion.

Stage posts

Stage posts are the points at which progress is reviewed and changes made, if necessary, in the blueprints and the worksheets. As each stage post is reached all aspects of the bridge-building exercise have to be examined. A good way to do this is to see how far across the 'performance gap' the bridge has reached, by looking at the way that expectations are being met, outcomes produced and results achieved.

Reviewing what we have achieved to date, i.e. 'what we have produced', is much better than focusing on the inputs to the bridge building, i.e. what we have been doing. If we are seduced by the appearance of hard work and much effort rather than the output of the effort we will lose sight of where we are going.

What we should be looking at is 'How far have we got?' not 'How much have we done?' All too often people focus on what has been done rather than what has been achieved and in the process change the blueprints to show declining aspirations in what is likely to be achieved. In other words the performance gap is closed by reducing expectations rather than by building bridges.

The three step approach – a way forward

The three steps to successfully bridging the 'performance gap' are:

- Identify the missing ingredients
- Measure the 'performance gap'
- Build performance bridges

This approach is not a once-and-for-all effort. It is a continuous approach that needs to be built into an effective performance management system. The way to do this and the problems and pitfalls that will be met and overcome on the journey is what the rest of this book sets out to describe.

2 Measuring performance

Performance is not measured by 'what we bring' (competencies) or 'what we do', but by 'what we produce'. It is the outcome and the results of our efforts. This means that measuring performance is a matter of measuring outcomes and results – the 'output focus' – and is fundamental to creating an effective performance management system.

Using an input focus on 'what we bring' and 'what we do' does not lead directly to improved performance and only serves to take the spotlight away from what we should be measuring. Imagine measuring the performance of high jumpers by the way they run up and their competency to leap, rather than the height they clear.

Focusing on outputs

Stating 'what we produce' is of little value if it is not clear 'how' it can be achieved and measured. This depends on finding answers to four important questions.

- What is the output (outcomes and results) of the activity?
- How can the output be measured?
- Can outputs be related directly to inputs?
- How can outputs be improved?

In order to maintain an 'output focus' we have to provide criteria for measuring outcomes and results. This is where the first and perhaps the most significant difficulty in measuring performance arises. Let's examine the outcomes and results for the team development programme mentioned in Chapter 1.

Outcomes	*Results*
1 Improved communications	Improved morale
2 Ownership of decisions	Improved profits
3 Sharing workloads	Improved working environment
4 Asking for help	Reduced stress

These outcomes and results are easy to state and seem perfectly valid for the project concerned. But how can we measure them? This is the important question. If we cannot measure them, what is the value of stating them in the first place? Without clear measurement criteria they are nothing more than a wish list.

People sometimes focus exclusively on the results achieved, but this is only part of the answer. I recently watched a football match on television. Newcastle United managed to secure a win that their performance didn't merit. Afterwards Kevin Keegan, manager of Newcastle, said: 'After such a poor performance we were lucky to get a result'.

It is not sufficient to establish criteria for measuring results; we have to be able to measure the extent to which the outcomes have been produced. This will depend on many factors including the organization and the specific circumstances.

The measurements used in the team development project were agreed as follows:

Outcomes

Improved communications

- Memos produced by the team (both paper and e-mail based) to be halved.
- Number and duration of meetings to be halved.
- Phone calls between team members to be halved.
- Face-to-face contact between team members outside meetings to be doubled.

Ownership of decisions

- A decision analysis to be completed indicating who takes which decisions.
- Decision delays to be eliminated (decisions taken within time scale agreed on the decision analysis).
- Decision involvement only in accordance with the decision analysis.

Sharing workloads

- Record of work done with/for each other.
- Record of times cover undertaken for each other.

Asking for help

- Record of requests made.
- Record of requests received.

Where the measures were against the current levels these were analysed to form the benchmark for improvement. Each member of the team was asked to keep a simple daily/diary record of all relevant measures.

Results

Improved morale

- More time available to accommodate the needs of others.
- Attitude survey of members of the management team's immediate work group (staff) (taken before the programme started and again at 3 months and 6 months).
- Reduced working hours of team members (at the start average working week was 70 hours).

Improved profits

- Change between profit expectations for the next 6 months at start of the programme and actual profits for the 6 months.

Improved working environment

- All team members have space in their diaries for contact with each other (one hour a day open for this purpose).
- Attitude survey of team members at start of programme and at 3 months and 6 months.

Reduced stress

- Physical measures from medical examination of items such as weight, blood pressure, cholesterol, symptoms such as headaches, stiff necks, etc.
- Temperament questionnaire dealing with feelings about work and contact with others (taken at start of programme and at 3 months and 6 months).

Many of the measures used in this particular example were decided upon as meaningful and relevant in the circumstances. For example, all the team had an annual medical examination and stress had been indicated as a problem.

The important aspects of producing measures for outcomes and results are:

- Can the measures actually be taken?
- Are they thought to be meaningful by the people being measured?
- Are the people being measured involved in the measurement process?
- Can the measures be used on a continuous basis?
- Do they relate to corporate goals?

Relating outputs to inputs

In order to improve performance, i.e. achieve higher standards, we have to look at the 'critical performance factors' which were introduced in Chapter 1: the environment, the conditions, personal desires, personal state and personal competencies. This might appear as follows.

Example:	Serving customers	
Outputs:	Outcomes	– answering enquiries
		– providing the service the customer wants in an efficient friendly way
	Results	– satisfied customers
		– increase in customers

If we take the first of these outcomes, we can show the importance of each critical factor:

Output – answering enquiries

Critical factors

The environment	Quiet, confidential area
The conditions	Information to hand, no time pressure
Personal desires	Want to be helpful, want to be liked, want to be efficient
Personal state	Physically well, calm, contented
Personal competencies	Knowledge of subject, articulate, patient, good personal contact

Improving outputs

With the information of what might impact on the outputs of an activity it is possible to focus on each critical factor to see if there is any way in which they can be improved and thus produce an improvement in the outputs. In this way the analysis of activity outputs and the definition of performance measures can lead to the formulation of ideas for bridging the 'performance gap'.

Establishing performance indicators

Performance measures which can be related to each other in some way provide us with an opportunity to establish 'performance indicators'. Motor cars have various instruments which give the driver information, yet few vehicles have any performance indicators. Take, for example, use of fuel. Cars have a fuel gauge which measures the contents of the fuel tank. They also have a speedometer that tells drivers what speed they are travelling at, and a mileometer that records the distance travelled. By combining this information it is possible to display a 'performance indicator' of fuel consumption. Some cars have a digital display that rises and falls as more or less fuel is used, for example when accelerating. With such a performance indicator it would be possible to adjust driving to optimize fuel consumption.

If a particular activity had measures of performance for number of customers served and time spent per customer, it would be possible to devise a performance indicator that calculated and displayed this information. Of course where the extent of the services offered covers a wide range it might also be necessary to take into account the average amount spent by customers and the particular services provided. It might then be possible to provide performance indicators for:

number of customers per hour
average time per customer
average customer spend
range of services provided.

Performance indicators are a way of combining measures of performance output to indicate the current level being achieved. If it is possible to produce a single performance indicator for an activity, then it might also be possible to monitor this continuously and provide feedback so that action and behaviour can be adjusted to optimize performance.

It may not always be possible to produce performance indicators for activities, but the search is well worthwhile. When they are produced they can have a very significant and beneficial effect on performance levels.

Establishing standards

Standards are the desired or intended levels of achievement that can be set for performance measures and performance indicators. In the examples discussed above we could set the standard for the performance indicator of customers per hour of between 15–20, and the standard for the performance measure of customer spend as £30–£50.

Setting standards is rarely straightforward. If they are set too high then failure to perform to standard will demotivate people, if set too low then poor performance becomes acceptable. Perhaps the best approach is to set standards within a range from minimum acceptable to maximum expected.

If we set standards as a range of performance then it is possible to take account of variations in all the critical factors that might affect performance and still ensure high overall levels of performance. There is no doubt that performance will fluctuate as the critical factors vary. To ignore this is to ignore the obvious and yet many organizations, all too readily, set standards which are impossible to achieve and inflexible.

Standards and targets

There is a great deal of misunderstanding and misuse of the terms 'standard' and 'target'. A standard as described above is a range of desirable and/or intended performance. A target is something to be aimed for and could be set above the standard range.

We might have a standard range of customer service of between 15–20 per hour and a target of 25. We might have a standard for customer spend as £30–£50 and a target of £65. It is then possible to reward people in relation to both levels of performance and achievement of targets over and above performance standards.

There is a danger in using targets as a way of increasing performance levels, which is the possible fall in quality standards. It is important that performance standards are set not only for measures of volume of work, but also for the quality factors attached to the activity concerned. This means that when considering the outputs and the measures appropriate for each activity we have to make sure that they include both volume and quality measures.

The aim should be to create a situation where people are able to focus on outputs and to have measures and indicators for that output that are meaningful and achievable.

Performance assessment – the components

We cannot assess performance unless we have some idea about the expected outputs and the standards we are looking for and the current nature of the critical performance factors. So the components for performance assessment are:

- expected outcomes and results
- performance measures and indicators for each
- performance standards
- targets (where appropriate)
- actual performance achieved
- nature of the critical factors.

With all these components it is possible to assess the extent of the performance gap and to have some ideas about the contributing factors. This in turn leads on to action for bridging the performance gap.

3 The critical performance factors

One of the key problems in many performance management systems is that they focus on 'how well' people have done, or have failed to do, rather than focusing on 'how much better' they could do and what needs to happen to make this possible. It is important to assess and recognize how far people have got and what they have achieved. People need good feedback about their performance. This is the starting point for going further. However, it should not be the only, or the main, focus. The aim of performance management in the broadest sense is to bridge the 'performance gap'. The focus should be on building bridges, and this means looking closely at the impact of the critical performance factors.

These factors, briefly mentioned in Chapter 1, are: the environment; the conditions; personal desires; personal state and personal competencies.

The environment

The working environment has a great impact on people's performance. Consider for a moment the environment that you work in. Would you say it is the perfect environment to support your performance? You can probably think of some ways in which it could be improved.

There are six aspects of the environment which should be carefully considered when designing 'high performance' settings:

- The *space* that you occupy and its location. You should have enough space to work in comfort, with the services of lighting, heating, air conditioning (or preferably fresh air) and privacy if you need it (or access to private space when you need it). There are moves towards creating environments where people use space as they need it and don't have their own particular workplace. This is fine as long as the space is designed to support high performance.

- The *facilities* that you have available including power, connection to networks, access to refreshments, access to toilets, telecoms, fax, photocopying, stationery and so on. All these facilities should be within easy and quick access appropriate for the work being done.
- The *equipment* that you need should be within easy reach and for most people today this means a computer terminal and a telephone, either desk top or portable. It can also mean machinery, forklift trucks, motor vehicles, and whatever is needed to ensure high performance of the specific tasks.
- The *support* you need from colleagues and management should be available in terms of help and advice when you need it, as well as sharing your workload and covering for you when necessary. This is one aspect of creating a good working environment which is most frequently missing. It is often the 'missing ingredient' that we are looking for.
- *Access* to your working environment should be easy with the minimum of stress and difficulty in getting there. This could mean good car parking or public transport, and/or being able to work from home if possible. Unfortunately we are still living in a world where 'people go to work' instead of 'work going to people'. Paying attention to this aspect so that people arrive at work fresh and stress free can have a significant impact on performance.
- *Contact* with other people is the final part of the environment factor, if possible face-to-face contact with the people you are working closest with. Contact with people via telecoms, e-mail etc. is useful when they are located at some distance, but using these methods when working down the corridor does not make for good supportive contact.

It is clear from this brief summary of six aspects of the environment factor that it is going to be very difficult to create an ideal environment for creating high performance. There is nearly always an 'environment gap' to be bridged.

The conditions

The conditions in which people are expected to perform are often so poor that it is amazing they are able to achieve even the lowest levels, but somehow they do. Because of this human capacity to triumph over adversity people are expected to tolerate very limiting conditions. There are five important aspects of working conditions:

- *Freedom* to perform in a way best suited to each of us is a rare commodity.

It seems that 'others' know better how we can perform than we do ourselves. We are expected to produce our best whilst paying attention to all kinds of rules and instructions and with a constant need to check back and upwards for decisions. It is important to have boundaries to what people are free to do, but they should be as few as possible and enable people to operate with the greatest degree of initiative and freedom (see Chapter 17).

- *Responsibility* is an appropriate balance for freedom. By clearly attributing responsibility to activities and tasks it is possible to provide the freedom people need. When you are responsible for what you are doing and you have the freedom to do it to the best of your ability you have the conditions necessary for high performance. If managers are held responsible for what people do it is difficult for these managers to give their people the freedom to perform. Instead they have to monitor what they do and 'control' what is happening. The result is poor performance.
- *Boundaries and limits* that are imposed on people do not simply have the effect of limiting performance, they also limit the risks to the organization of the responsibilities they give to their people. One example of this balance between setting boundaries and giving people an unlimited scope is the famous case of Nick Leeson and Barings Bank, where a trader was able to commit the bank to massive losses. The answer is to find the balance that enables high performance within agreed boundaries.
- Providing *learning and coaching* on a continuous basis for people is an essential precondition for high performance. People grow and benefit from constant attention to their learning and to their performance. Paying attention and being interested in what people are doing is an excellent way to motivate them especially if the focus is on their development.
- *Challenging* working opportunities in a supportive environment will provide people with the conditions they need to expand their capabilities and confidence, which is not the same as 'throwing them in at the deep end'. It is more akin to taking them up a steep rock face whilst they are securely roped onto and guided by experienced rock climbers. The experience is challenging and exhilarating and yet they are protected.

Personal desires

Although the factor of personal desires is given such prominence in the sports world, it is almost ignored in the business world. It is as though they are considered irrelevant to the question of performance. Nothing could be further from the truth. The seven aspects of this factor of performance discussed below are not an exhaustive list, but they are the most pertinent.

- *Self-satisfaction* is of paramount importance to all performers. To finish the day feeling satisfied with what has happened and the way you have performed is a wonderful feeling. Paradoxically it is often much harder to satisfy yourself than other people. If you start your day by imagining what you want to do to satisfy yourself you will probably try to cram far too much into every hour. On the other hand, if you try to achieve some sense of self-satisfaction as the day proceeds you will probably manage to do it. If self-satisfaction is hard to achieve or is missing altogether then it becomes an important part of the 'missing ingredient' we are searching for.

- *Belonging* to a group of people, a department, or a team is an important aspect of 'personal desire'. If people feel that they belong they are more likely to cooperate and help others in their group. They will feel more at ease and therefore more able to perform at their best. The opposite of belonging is to feel isolated and rejected and such a state will not contribute to the individual's performance.

- When people have a high sense of their *self-value* they are not looking to score 'brownie points' or to increase their sense of worth by minimizing the work of others. They are able to concentrate on getting on with their job in a confident way and performing at their best. People with a low self-value tend to be constantly unsure and in need of support, encouragement and affirmation of what they are doing. They seem to lack confidence and hence don't perform at their best.

- We all want to *grow and develop* in the widest sense and so we will respond better in an atmosphere which clearly supports our personal growth and development. Most organizations recognize this basic human need and respond to it. Unfortunately they do so with the focus only on the current job the person is doing, or on preparing people for their next step up the ladder. The growth and development of people in the widest context is usually left for them to do on their own outside working hours. This is due to a misunderstanding about people and performance. You cannot separate specific attributes of people which apply to their jobs as if the rest of the person is not present. To get the very best performance the totality of the person has to be attended to.

- Being *good at what you do* is a crucial aspect of your performance. It means that you have confidence, a good sense of self-value and that you are trusted and given freedom to get on with your job. When you move on to doing something new and different you are for a time not good at what you do. You are in a learning mode. The expectations placed on you in these circumstances should reflect this temporary situation and you should be appreciated for being good at learning. If you are not good at what you do and not respected as a learner you will very soon receive negative feedback. Your self-value will fall. You will not be self-satisfied and your performance will deteriorate. Dealing with people who are not good at what they do is one of management's most intractable problems, mainly because managers are not good at it.

● People need *respect* from colleagues, managers, and others that they come into contact with. Respect simply means treating people as you want to be treated. I was working with a group of people to help them to improve their customer service skills. I asked them to describe how they liked to be treated when they were a customer and to produce a definition of customer service. The outcome was a clear and simple statement of good customer service. The same is true of respect. We all know when we are being respected and when we are not.

● To perform at your very best you need the freedom *to be yourself*. There is much talk of diversity in the workplace without a great deal of understanding of what it means. Diversity means acceptance of all your differences without demanding that you conform to some way of being that is alien to you. Only when you can be fully who you are can you call on all your talents to perform at your very best.

Personal state

Our personal state changes from moment to moment. It is affected by climate, the atmosphere, what is happening to us in our lives, our relationships, whether we are happy or sad, tired or energetic, what is happening to people close to us, and many other aspects of our daily living. It is impossible to ignore the effect of our personal state on our performance, yet some organizations do try to ignore it.

● Our *physical state* has the most apparent effect – if we feel bad enough we don't even go to work. We don't attempt to perform. When we are not 'sick' enough to take time off our performance still suffers. Careful attention is often paid to physical welfare and people are encouraged to look after themselves. It is not unusual to find organizations which are 'non-smoking' and which have their own fitness centres. Regular medicals may be offered to senior (older) people and stress levels are monitored.

● Our *psychological state* is not so apparent and is not so well cared for. Organizations are increasingly providing counselling services for staff with 'problems'. Unfortunately people don't like to admit having problems, especially psychological ones, though this attitude is changing. The impact our psychological state can have on our performance is just as great as our physical state. Allowing people a day off to attend a close relative's funeral might seem helpful, but a bereaved person needs much more time to grieve and even if they come to work their performance is considerably affected. This is a typical example of ignoring psychological issues. Ignoring the psychological needs of a new father also leads to considerable fall off in performance. Because of this paternity leave is now becoming a feature of the welfare provisions of some organizations.

- *Congruency* occurs when people are in tune with what they are doing. It is based on the honest expression of feelings in a way that is real and consistent with events. When you are angry if you say in a quiet voice, 'No, it is OK I'm fine, I'm not angry', then you're being incongruent, dishonest and avoiding dealing with your real feeling. A congruent response would be to say, 'Yes, I am angry, I am very angry and I want to scream, but I am not going to'. When we are not congruent we suppress how we feel and, contrary to what we say, we are angry inside and dwell on the event long after it is over. The result is that we perform in a half-hearted way because half of us is still dealing with the unexpressed feelings. By acknowledging our true feelings and expressing them we release them and we are then able to return to perform unencumbered.

Personal competencies

People have a vast range of competencies that they have learned during their lives from all of their experiences, but which are not always fully acknowledged by organizations. The focus becomes 'competencies for the job'. This is understandable to some extent but it is a very limiting attitude. It tends to cause people to exclude competencies from their work when in fact these might be valuable.

- *Competencies for the job* are those attributes that have been defined as necessary to do the job. They include: knowledge (what you need to know); skills (what you need to be able to do); attitudes (the way that you think about your work) and behaviour (how you respond to the situations that arise in your work). When people are able to display these attributes they are deemed to be 'competent'. Arriving at this position involves a learning curve for each new situation and learning becomes a key aspect of developing competency.
- *Competencies for life* are often ignored when looking at performance. As with congruency you cannot have part of a person without having all of

the person. The woman who is a customer service officer might also be a wife, a mother, director of the amateur dramatic society, captain of the hockey team, speak three languages, lead climbing expeditions and be a competent skier. To say that these competencies do not impact on this woman's performance is ridiculous, and it is equally so to pretend that she does not bring them with her as part of herself when she is at work.

● What is true of competencies is also true of our *experiences*. When we focus only on work-based experiences we limit both people and the potential that they bring to the job. One very limiting question is: 'Have you had any relevant experience?' What does this mean? Does it mean, 'Have you done this before?' or 'Have you done something similar before?' Surely a better approach would be to ask: 'What experience have you had that makes you think you can do the job?' All our experiences are relevant to everything we do.

● Our *capabilities* are how well we use our competencies and experience in what we do. It means that you can apply your abilities in a wide variety of different situations and use your initiative in a confident way. You seem self-assured and it is likely that your performance will be good. You can only be capable if you bring your complete self to work and if you are respected for who you are as well as for what you do.

● *Talents* are those particular abilities which transcend competency and become something much more exciting and creative. Talents, when they are known about and appreciated, can be harnessed for work-based performance in a surprisingly effective and valuable way. Here is one example. A young man working as an engineering apprentice was also a talented rock climber and at the age of twenty was leading alpine expeditions during his holidays. When this information came to light (he was reluctant to talk about his talent at work) he was invited to talk to a group of supervisors and managers about what it was like to lead a team of climbers. With the help of the training manager he prepared a slide show and talk, which was later converted into a team leadership programme and resulted in the young man taking a group of managers on a development programme in the Welsh mountains.

Performance barriers

In addition to those performance factors which need to be present to enable high performance to take place, there are also barriers which can get in the way of people performing at their very best. Removing these barriers is easier when people are aware of their existence and acknowledge the degree to which they affect performance.

- *The lack of applause,* acknowledgement, recognition and appreciation is a distinct and common barrier to performance. It is as if there is a reluctance to applaud someone for a good performance. In the book *The One Minute Manager*[1] there is a suggestion that it is a good idea 'to catch people doing things right'.

  It is difficult to say why people, especially managers, are reluctant to applaud good performers. Perhaps there is a sense of 'I have not been applauded for what I do, so I am not going to applaud you'. This ungenerous and mean-spirited approach is a definite barrier to high performance.

  You can remove this barrier by making sure that applause is widely and often given for high performance, so much so that it becomes a regular and welcome part of the culture to applaud others.

- *Unfinished business* is a barrier to performance because it hinders subsequent attempts to complete something. When we are attending to some task there is a natural flow from starting to completing the activity. If this flow is interrupted so that we don't reach completion, we are left with some unfinished business. This is frustrating and the incomplete activity prevents us from continuing what we want to do next. Needless to say this causes stress and tension and can lead to us behaving 'inappropriately'.

  Imagine that you have recently had a row with someone close to you and it is unresolved. There will be a continuing tension until you can resolve the issue and complete the natural cycle. If during this time an issue arises with a colleague at work it is likely that the feelings attached to the unresolved row will spill over into your contact with your colleague. You might be angry with them, or burst into tears over the slightest criticism. In other words the self-regulating mechanism that is searching for completion of the previous event can affect the 'here and now' way in which you behave and substantially reduce your performance.

  The barrier of unfinished business can be removed by being aware of what is unfinished and trying to complete it as soon as possible. Alternatively the unfinished business can be held safely in pending until it can be completed.

- *The lack of enjoyment* is a significant barrier to high performance because if you have to do something that you don't enjoy doing your natural desire to do it, except to get it over as soon as possible, is just not there. If, on the other hand, you enjoy what you are doing, you are much more likely to be successful and to perform well. There is a very strong link between 'being good at what you enjoy' and 'enjoying what you are good at'.

  Lack of enjoyment can be removed by acknowledging openly what you do and do not enjoy so that if you have to do something that you do not enjoy it is clear that your performance will be affected and vice versa.

- *Envy* is a very real barrier to performance. People who envy the high performance of others may strive to emulate them. They may also strive to interfere with and denigrate those who are the cause of their envy. Those who are envied may dislike the reaction of the people who envy them and may reduce their performance to remove the apparent cause of the envy.

    It is very difficult to remove the envy barrier to performance. Perhaps the best approach is to be aware that it is a barrier and to recognize and name it for what it is when it does appear.

A learning environment

This chapter has focused on the critical performance factors that contribute to and/or get in the way of high performance. Attention to these factors is the best way to clearly define the 'performance gap' and to determine the 'missing ingredients'. For this work to be successful it has to be done in a 'learning environment' – one which pays attention to the following components.

Cooperation NOT competition

When people compete it is believed that there is a drive to higher performance. The desire to win can increase performance. It can also reduce performance. Imagine a 5000 metre race. If the aim is to win it can be achieved in a relatively slow time depending on the others in the race. If the aim is to beat the world record then the chosen person will need the cooperation of the other runners to provide a fast early pace. In other words competition does not always lead to the best performance, whereas cooperation nearly always does.

Support NOT supervision

Good performers need support not supervision. If supervision is replaced by coaching which is based on support then higher levels of achievement will be reached. Supervision tends to involve monitoring and direction and some form of external impetus for the performer. People learn from coaching. Of course this is using the term 'supervision' in the context of 'looking over the shoulder'. If supervision is seen more as 'super-vision', seeing more clearly, then it becomes more akin to coaching which is fine as long as it supports the performer in what they are doing.

Feedback NOT criticism

Feedback is a fundamental part of the high performance environment, and is covered in more detail in Chapter 6. Suffice it to say here that giving non-critical feedback is an important aspect of assessing and reporting performance and, of course, learning.

Enjoyment NOT pressure

If it is possible to maintain a high level of enjoyment people both learn and perform. Pressure may appear to drive people to performance, but only if the external energy, i.e. the source of the pressure, is applied with great sensitivity so that the experience is still enjoyable. Usually pressure is exerted in a way that is totally out of control and removes any and all sense of enjoyment, even from the success that might be achieved. One problem is the widely held belief that work is too serious to be enjoyed.

Reference

1   Blanchard, K. and Johson, S., *The One Minute Manager*, Collins, London, 1983.

4 Organismic learning

It is a great fallacy that adults learn differently from young children. It has been born out of the apparent ways that adults seem to process information and respond to stimuli. However, what we see is not the natural development of the human organism. Because what we see in adults is different from what we believe we see in children we have interpreted this to mean that the human organism of the adult functions differently from that of a child. Adults do indeed do things differently from young children, but this is only because the life experiences of the adult have introduced barriers to the creative learning functions we are born with. In other words the power of the adult human organism to learn has been interfered with. The latent holistic learning power of the newborn infant has been repressed and constrained by years of conditioning so that it is no longer available to most adults.

Imagine the time when you first learned to ride a bike. Did you receive lectures on the inherent instability of the device? Were you given information about the laws of aerodynamics, of balance, gravity etc? Were the potential dangers and possible pain of the learning experience spelt out to you? No. None of this happened. You just sat on the bike and had a wobbly go with someone supporting you. You probably fell off. You probably got back on undeterred. Eventually you had a go without support and then, miraculously, you could do it. Without knowing anything about balance you could balance. Without knowing anything about aerodynamics and force you could negotiate corners and make the inherently unstable device stable. But how was this possible? How could so much learning take place without you knowing what you were doing?

The answer is remarkably simple. Our organism in its wholeness has the power to learn from experience. It does this whether or not we are aware of it. Our bodies can make imperceptible muscular adaptations so that each time we fall off the bike the organism automatically adjusts to compensate.

When enough experience has occurred the organism has learned, not as a separate brain, body, mind, but as an integrated whole.

Young children learning to ski are not given information about the shape of the ski as adults are. How does it help to know that the 'cut' making the ski narrower at the waist is what makes the ski turn. It doesn't, but some instructors think adults need to know. The reason young children just go and do it is exactly because they are free of unnecessary information and can rely on their inherent organismic learning power, and have great fun whilst doing so. In addition they are not afraid of falling down, or failing as adults might well call it. In fact the term 'falling down on the job' is frequently used by adults in a derogatory way. Young children might say, 'But that is silly. How can you learn unless you fall down?'.

When we learn to trust our inherent organismic learning power, in an appropriately supportive environment, we can truly create miracles. We can take our first steps to bridging the performance gap. So let's start here taking the first wobbly steps towards helping people to rediscover and release their learning power.

Go out and buy yourself a set of three juggling balls and learn to juggle. Don't make it a goal, just do it for fun. It takes a few minutes, maybe half-an-hour to learn. (I juggle now and then for a few minutes to remind me that I possess a wonderful organismic learning power.)

There are ten keys to opening the doors behind which we have locked away a veritable treasure-trove. They are not rigid rules, but are reminders to trust our organismic learning power. They help us to present learning opportunities to others in such a way as to remind them of their own learning power. They are keys of empowerment which help to show people the path to their own wisdom rather than trying to share with them the little wisdom we have. As you explore each key remember that you already knew what I was going to say before I said it, but didn't know that you did until after I said it.

1   Mistakes are a basis for learning, not a reason for criticism

I have learned throughout my life as a composer chiefly through my mistakes and pursuits of false assumptions, not by my exposure to founts of wisdom and knowledge.

Igor Stravinsky[1]

What was true for Stravinsky is true for each of us, but often we don't realize the importance of this self-evident truth. Each time you make a mistake you have an opportunity to learn, but this is lost if you are criticized because of the mistake.

'Look what you've done now. Good grief, don't you know any better? This is going to cause real problems.' This reaction to your mistake is more likely to elicit an apology and make you feel foolish than to help you to learn. It might also encourage you to avoid the experience in the future for fear of eliciting the same or an even worse response.

'OK, so that's not exactly what we wanted. Let's look at what happened and what you did.' This reaction acknowledges the mistake, but focuses on the opportunity that it presents to examine what happened and to learn from it. It demands no apology; it is not threatening, and doesn't carry blame.

You might be thinking: 'This is OK up to a point, but what about the person who keeps making the same mistake?' A good question, which could be changed to: 'What about the support the person is receiving to help them learn?' In my experience people who repeatedly make mistakes have not received support and encouragement during their learning.

I recall one young woman who was having difficulty with a particular computer procedure. Her supervisor told me: 'She just doesn't understand. I must have explained it ten times to her. It really frustrates me.' I spoke to the woman and then showed her what to do on the machine. I asked her to watch me and then tell me what she saw. When we had finished she said: 'But it is so easy, no one showed me before'.

When people for whose work you are responsible make a mistake, remember these four steps:

- acknowledge the mistake non-critically
- find out from them what happened
- show them what to do
- ask them to demonstrate that they can do it.

Stay with this cycle of activity until they are happy that they can do it in the required way.

2   Unwanted information obscures more than it illuminates

'OK,' he said, taking his ski pole and drawing a curve in the snow, 'this is the line of the turn. Now here where I have marked the cross is the sweet point of the turn. As you approach the turn, place your pole on the inside of the line at the sweet point and at the same time transfer your weight onto what becomes the downhill ski.'

To say I was confused would not be true. I understood the words the instructor had spoken, but I was having some difficulty in converting them into any sensible message for my arms, legs, hips and knees. There was a distinct gap between what I had heard and what I could do. This feeling was confirmed as soon as I tried to do it.

The desire to give information as a primary step in the learning process is endemic in our education system, and it is as ineffective as it is boring. The wonderful organism we call a human being works in a different way, and this is true at all ages. As we experience something if we want information we ask for it. We do this because we need to fill a gap between our current knowledge and the experience we are having. When we have the information the gap is filled and we can continue with the experience. If we are given information before the experience, we don't know which bit is relevant or useful to us. We have to store it all in some way unrelated to our existing knowledge. If we don't soon find a use for it, we will discard it.

So instead of giving people information about what they are learning we present them with exercises and problems to solve. As they do this they will need information which we can give to them in a way which is useful and thus encourage learning. We do in fact feed questioning minds.

A man has no ears for that to which experience has given him no access.

Nietzsche[2]

Have you ever had to eat a meal when you weren't hungry? It's the same feeling as being given information you do not want, and cannot use.

3   We can do things without knowing how

There is a mistaken belief, usually in the minds of those who teach or train adults, that people have to know how to do something before doing it. Unfortunately many adults have picked up this message via the education system and now think this is true for them. It is not. It is perfectly possible to do things without 'knowing' how.

For example, Neil, a car salesman, produced one of the best closes of a sale I have ever witnessed. An elderly man and his wife were dithering about buying the car that they obviously liked. Neil said: 'I can see that you're not sure, and the last thing I want you to do is buy a car you're not sure about. You would never be happy, and worse still you would not come back to buy another car from me. I suggest you go home and think about it and come back when you are sure.' Neil came over to speak to me and the couple stood talking animatedly together. After about ten minutes the man came over and said: 'Neil, we've decided. You were quite right, we weren't sure, but we are now. We want to go ahead.' When the couple had left I asked Neil where he had learned to close sales in such a brilliant way. 'Do what?' he asked. I explained what I had seen. 'Oh, so that's what I did, is it? Well, it just seemed the best thing to do to me,' was his somewhat surprised reply. I could easily call Neil a natural salesman because he seems to be able to do it without knowing what he is doing.

But even for people who are not 'naturals', it is possible to learn to do things without 'knowing' what they are doing. You can do this by copying someone else. You can do it by seeing what is being done from different perspectives, i.e. learn about serving customers by experiencing what it is like to be a customer.

Rather than 'knowing' how, try to provide opportunities in which people can 'discover' how. Do you remember learning to tie your own shoelaces? You were shown how to do it and through experience you discovered how to do it. I doubt if you could explain it from your knowledge very easily, but you can do it.

4 Experience provides our primary source of learning

The child is curious. He wants to make sense of things. Find out how things work. Gain competence and control over himself and his environment. Do what he can see other people doing. He is receptive, open and perceptive. He does not shut himself off from the strange, confused, complicated world around him. He observes it closely and sharply. Tries to take it all in. He is experimental. He does not merely observe the world around him but tastes it, touches it, hefts it, breaks it, bends it, to find out how reality works he works on it. He is bold. He is not afraid of making mistakes. And he is patient. He can tolerate an extraordinary amount of uncertainty, confusion, ignorance and suspense. He does not have to have instant meaning in any new situation. He is willing and able to wait for meaning to come to him – even if it comes slowly, which it usually does.

John Holt[3]

What do we, in this society of ours, do to kill this free-spinning organismic exploration of our experience? To encapsulate this experimental fervour and thirst for learning into the straitjacket of conventional ideas about being taught what we ought to know? Not only does it kill off our desire to learn, it patently slows down and prevents the rapid growth we are all capable of.

Helping people to learn is much more a process of providing them with appropriate experience in a framework of support than it is with any process of telling them or 'teaching' them.

A few years ago I was 'teaching' undergraduates managerial economics. At the first of my 'lectures' ninety students gathered in a tiered lecture theatre. They looked bored before we started. I stood and waited until they were quiet, which took about five minutes (later I was told that this in itself was somewhat unusual). I said that as the subject could be very dry and boring, I was going to offer them the opportunity to learn from experience, and that if this didn't work for them we could return to lectures. I then suggested we should start by working on takeovers and mergers. I would divide them into two different companies (I chose existing large companies). Then each of the company groups would divide into three groups – merchant bankers, directors and shareholders. This took about fifteen minutes for them to organize. I asked for a spokesperson for each of the six groups who then gave me the names of the people in their group. When this was completed I had ninety curious and highly attentive students. 'OK,' I said, 'now I want company X to make a takeover bid for company Y.' A buzz of conversation went round the group, then one of the spokespersons asked me how they were to do it. I suggested several books they could read and some articles in recent publications and told them to get on with it. I also said that I was available to answer questions from spokespersons, and that the tutor groups would be each of the six groups.

The four periods allocated to takeovers and mergers were lively, fun and highly educative. In fact we covered more ground than I would ever have dared to try to cover in four lectures. They discovered what they needed to know, they enjoyed it, worked cooperatively, and rediscovered their learning power.

5   All our past experience and learning is relevant to every new experience we face

I met a young man, Ken, in the course of helping to prepare school leavers for attending job interviews. I had an application form that Ken had completed. There were no details about his skills as a leader or his ability to influence people. However, I noticed in the section on the form for pastimes a reference to youth work. I asked him what this was and he described how he worked with a group of disabled young people taking them for trips and supervising them swimming. He was also a group leader for the other volunteers he worked with. To do all this he had to have considerable leadership skills, and he was obviously capable of engendering trust in others. I asked him why he had made so little of it in his application form. 'Oh, my parents told me not to go on about my activities with the youth group as it wasn't relevant to work.'

Nothing that we have experienced in the past is irrelevant. We may not be able to reason why it is relevant, but it is because it is a part of determining who we are today. There are numerous examples of people who have compartmentalized their experience in such a way that one part is not available to them when they are doing something in another part of their lives.

Helping people to learn involves exploring with them the extent of their past learning, and inviting them to bring all of it to bear on their current experience.

6   We are always in control of our own learning

At all times and in all situations we choose to learn what we learn or, if you prefer, choose not to learn when it suits us. No matter how a learning opportunity presents itself, or is presented to us, we make a decision whether and what to learn. Sometimes we may not be conscious of this choice taking place, but it does. No one knows exactly what happens as we exercise this control over our learning, but here are a few ideas:

We decide we have no use for this learning.
We have already learned this.
This doesn't interest us/we are bored.
We don't respect/like you, so we won't learn from you.
We don't comprehend what's going on.
We are distracted.

There may be many more reasons why we choose not to learn, but these are not of interest to us now. We are interested in why people choose to learn something. Perhaps

We have to because …
We want to because we can use it.
We are interested.
It is fun.
It is exciting.
It seems like a good idea.
It may be useful to us in the future.
We respect/like you, so we want to learn from you.

Again this is not an exhaustive list and you can probably add other reasons why you choose to learn. The important point is that if we don't help people to think about why they want to learn what we are helping them to learn, they may choose not to learn it.

7   Demonstration is more powerful than description

'You can build a pyramid from these four identical pieces of wood by placing them in pairs so that the rectangular sides are adjacent forming a square. Then take one pair and invert them through 180 degrees so that the square formed by the two rectangular sides sits on top of the same square on the other pair.'

I have given this description to numerous audiences who have the four wooden blocks in front of them. Even if they hear me and understand my description, most of them have great difficulty in doing it within the two minutes allocated. Even when I give them the information on a screen to read they still have difficulty. But after I have demonstrated it to them without any words, they can all do it within the allotted twenty seconds.

I can hear some of you saying: 'That's OK with a visual and tactile problem, but what about intellectual problems that I can't demonstrate?' I have not yet met such a problem that could not be demonstrated through some physical analogy or metaphor. Here is an example.

In my managerial economics class we had to discuss inflation and its impact on the economy. Whether or not you have studied economics, think of the word 'inflation' in contexts other than economics and I am sure you can come up with a suitable analogy or metaphor. I used the idea of a balloon and with this simple device I demonstrated inflation, deflation and overheating of the economy.

You have to be creative to demonstrate. You have to innovate to demonstrate. It is easier to describe, but harder for others to learn from your description.

8   Experimentation is more powerful than explanation

After a demonstration it is more effective to invite people to have a go than it is to explain what you think they saw. Of course it is important to make sure the environment in which the experiment takes place is protective of the learners.

It may even be a good idea to ask people to experiment before you demonstrate to them. In this way they will often be more attentive during the demonstration, or other form of learning experience.

I was asked by a bank to look at the way junior managers learned to analyse balance sheets before agreeing to loans to small businesses. The course they were following had a section at the beginning which described the elements of the balance sheet. This was followed by a session on calculating balance sheet ratios, and then another on interpreting the ratios. This is a typical example of giving people information before they know what it is for, or why they need it.

I suggested that we should change the programme and start with an example of a company balance sheet and ask them to analyse it and make a recommendation about lending. By doing this the junior managers would discover what they did and didn't know and be more aware of the need for some analysis tools. And by being more aware they would be more willing and able to learn about and use them. The course developers were adamant that it wouldn't work, but we did it anyway to see, i.e. we experimented.

The first pilot programme ran and the outcome (I hesitate to say it was what I expected) showed that when presented with the problem these resourceful young managers obtained and studied appropriate texts from the course materials and presented well argued cases, including correctly worked ratio analysis. These were then discussed in a very energetic group session. In a much shorter space of time, with no lectures, and with little guidance except the materials, they had done a very good job of learning.

Every piece of learning can be developed as an experiment, but be prepared to construct the appropriate environment. The more innovative the experiment the better.

9   We take in sounds and images more effectively and faster than words

Words are symbols of things we see, hear, taste, touch and smell. We can use them to describe abstract concepts that we cannot experience with our senses. But our senses are still the primary source of most of the information our organism processes from its experience in the world.

Wherever possible we should make use of these powerful senses, just as the young child does, by creating sensory learning experiences. This is more often than you might expect.

The group of young people were together to learn about customer services. They all worked for the same bank. I had been asked to demonstrate to the trainers how a sensory experience could be built into the programme. I told the group to visit a branch of the bank as if they were a customer. 'I want you to concentrate on what you see, hear, touch, taste, and smell.' When I said this they all laughed. One of them asked me why? I told them that I believed we were affected as much by what we sensed as by what actually happens and what is said. I wanted them to experiment with this idea and then share their experiences.

The next day the group spent the morning at the bank. They assembled for lunch. They were very talkative over lunch and keen to return to the afternoon session. The feedback shocked both the group and the trainers. In summary what had been 'sensed' was a very noisy, unfriendly, untidy, dirty, smelly, and 'tasteless' environment. Staff were sensed as artificial, pretentious and patronizing. When the young people switched on their sensory perception they discovered what they, even working in the environment, had previously put out of awareness.

The result of this experiment was to include it in future programmes, and then to explore what could be done about it as part of a customer service approach when they returned to their branches.

10   Training is not learning

I have encountered the idea, particularly amongst trainers, that training provides people with knowledge and skills. It does not. Training provides people with an opportunity to learn. It is an input to the learning process. If it is particularly good and appropriate training, the outcome will be the 'desired' learning – desired because most training has an agenda, and is designed to produce certain prescribed learning outcomes. But, and it is an important but, learners will still choose to learn only what they want to learn.

So training is not learning, nor is it an indicator that learning has happened because people have undergone the training.

Training is the provision of effective meaningful learning opportunities. It includes providing courses, materials, experiences and practice in whatever is being learned. It is, or should be, designed to offer a variety of ways for participants to learn, and it should be clear about the expected outcomes.

The outcome of training is, or should be, learning. It usually takes the form of:

- enhanced knowledge about the subject
- some level of skill in the subject
- some desire to think differently (attitude change)
- some desire to act differently (behaviour change).

Helping people to learn may involve the use of training facilities and resources when appropriate, but this can only support the learning that takes place in the workplace as people endeavour to use the new knowledge and skills they have obtained. It is this phase of the process in which managers play such a vital role. Managers should encourage and support the learning of their people and provide an environment conducive to learning. Managers will find that the ten keys offered above will help to open the doors to the organismic learning power of those they want to help.

References

1 Stravinsky, I., *Themes and Episodes*, 1966.
2 Nietzsche, F., *Ecce Homo*, Penguin, Harmondsworth, 1992.
3 Holt, John, *How Children Learn*, Pelican Books, London, 1988.

5 Diversity and performance

People are unique

There is a strong link between diversity (recognition of individual uniqueness) and performance. If people are able to be fully themselves and to access and use all of their existing skills and potential, then they can perform at their very best.

I like to imagine people as shapes that depict their uniqueness. All the creativity and excitement is at the outer limits of their individualities and that is where they perform at their best. When people compress their 'spikiness' into some more acceptable form they limit themselves. When organizations demand such conformity they limit their people, and what becomes acceptable is represented by the central area of the diagram (see Figure 5.1).

This diagram represents an explosion of personal energy with the spikes being the outer reaches of the energy, where real contact is made with people

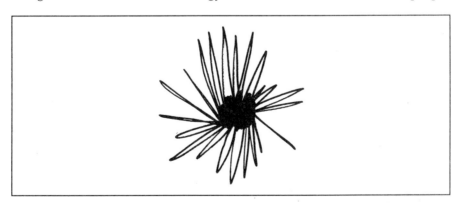

Figure 5.1   Personal energy flow

and the environment and where people 'perform to their limits'. If the energy is contained by social and organizational norms (culture) it is not available for people to access and use when they perform.

Because we are all different we will present different shapes to the world. Our energy will flow differently and our experiences, interests and desires will be different. One way of dealing with this is to try to limit and reduce difference by making people conform to some corporate image – creating a 'uniform' organization.

Uniform organizations

The uniform organization appears before us in banks, building societies, shops, airlines, travel agents, hotels, transport, utility suppliers, postman Pat and so on. The first impression is often a good one. Neat, smart and well turned out people give a surface impression of an efficient organization. They are recognizable as part of the organization to which they belong. The places they work, the vehicles they drive, all display the corporate identity that has cost a great deal of money to establish.

There are certain noticeable observations about uniform organizations. First, people rarely enjoy wearing the uniform which they are 'obliged' to wear. In fact the uniform is rarely named as such, but by euphemisms such as 'corporate wardrobe'. They are 'persuaded' that the uniform is a good thing because it is often subsidized and solves the problem of what to wear each day.

When asked how they feel about wearing the uniform they often answer with what sounds like the corporate doctrine for uniformity, identity, neatness etc. Sometimes people express their pride in belonging to the organization, being a part of such a company. These statements may sound sincere and heartfelt, but could they be a 'learned' response?

It is noticeable in uniform organizations that the 'rules' are often relaxed when people work away from the public gaze. This is especially true in Head Offices and corporate chiefs rarely, if ever, appear in the organization's uniform.

Staff in uniform organizations may often resent the loss of personal identity and seek other ways to display their individuality with hairstyles, jewellery, mascots etc. The wearing of badges or placing of nameplates on work stations is almost an essential feature of uniform organizations.

There is a noticeable sense of people having to work within tight constraints with many rules and procedures that have to be followed. It is as if the notion of uniformity has spread from how people appear to how they work. I heard one executive describe it as a consistent and recognizable way of doing business. Or, in other words, more of the same. Of course, customers have expectations and want them to be met, but supposing they get more than they bargained for? And what is the effect of always getting the same when it is below what is expected. Corporate identity only has a value when it is linked to high quality products and services.

Non-uniform organizations

Non-uniform organizations often display a more 'human' touch. People appear and behave more real, as equals, not as servants of the organization. They seem less constrained, friendlier and freer. I acknowledge that this impression might be because of some deep-seated prejudice I have towards uniforms and uniformity, but if I have such a prejudice then so do others.

The second point about non-uniform organizations is that there is often a very strong corporate identity on buildings, paperwork, vehicles etc. which does not extend to people. It is as if the organization recognizes that it does not own the people; that they are individuals who choose to work with the organization. I worked with one organization where staff could choose to wear a corporate tie-pin/button-hole/brooch, so that they could identify themselves with the organization if they wanted to. It was noticeable that all the senior directors and managers chose to wear the pins.

People in non-uniform organizations identify themselves as being with the organization by the way that they make contact with others. Your impression is of the person and the way they treat you. You have no sense that they are doing this for the organization, but rather that they are doing it for themselves. You are dealing at a personal level with another human being and not the organization's representative.

Whereas in the uniform organization you assess/judge that organization by the way you are treated by the person, in the non-uniform organization you assess/judge the person by the way they treat you. They clearly represent themselves first and the organization second. There is a big difference between letting the organization down and letting yourself down. This focus on self rather than organization is a much better basis for encouraging self-responsibility and improving quality of service, something which uniform organizations often miss out on altogether.

The final observation about non-uniform organizations is that people matter more. It is a question of seeing people rather than seeing the uniform. When this happens you are conscious that it is the people that matter, not what they represent, which in turn makes you feel as if you matter. You are not overwhelmed by the organization, not intimidated by its size and self-importance.

Experience shows that uniform organizations sacrifice the individual to the corporate colossus. They seek conformity and deference to the corporate image. They play down individuality and demand allegiance to the flag. Their corporate identity is what they stand for. It represents who they think they are. Everyone who works for the organization is expected to uphold these corporate values. They are expected to appear as members of the organization and whilst doing so to put the organization before themselves.

This presents people with a dilemma. Do they accept these corporate values because they believe them or because they want to keep their job? If they seek to express their individuality by being different they will stand out and probably have to get out. Do uniform organizations only attract those who are prepared to conform and put themselves second? Will uniform organizations lose the creativity that comes with diversity? Perhaps out of sight of the public gaze uniform organizations can encourage individuality, but this seems to go against such a strong need for corporate conformity that it is hard to imagine it happening.

Personal development

Let us return for a moment to the 'spiky' diagram (Figure 5.1) and to the way that development is often seen and approached. Along with the large powerful spikes there are areas of individuality represented by much smaller spikes. It is possible to see the large spikes as 'strengths' and the smaller spikes as 'weaknesses', but this is not helpful. The spikes represent differences that make people who they are. As people learn and experience life their shape changes. Some large spikes grow larger, others grow smaller, and some small spikes might increase in size or disappear altogether.

The process of personal development should focus not on deliberately changing someone's shape, but on adding to the whole and accepting whatever shape emerges. Enhancing strengths and correcting weaknesses is a very narrow view which might be relevant for a specialist athlete aiming for Olympic gold, but which is inappropriate for most of us.

Squashing potential

There is a basic human desire to belong which could mean that we choose not to stand out and possibly be rejected and isolated. We seek to hide our spikiness and to appear as the central, more limited conforming blob. This is a safe attitude and it limits us in all kinds of ways.

I am not attempting to suggest that we have conformity *or* diversity, but rather that it should be conformity *and* diversity in some appropriate balance. People need the comfort of belonging and being accepted which forms a base from which they can explore their difference.

This raises the issue of personal boundaries and about choosing what is appropriate diversity for each of us, and to what extent we seek the anonymity of conformity or risk the glare and isolation of difference.

As discussed above, some uniform organizations expect and/or demand conformity and I wonder whether or not it is this conformity which holds these organizations together. On balance I don't think that organizations would fall apart if they were to encourage people to be different. To what extent do individuals choose and develop their own level of conformity to create a culture they are comfortable with? This could in part explain why new people would be expected to 'fit' and not disturb the comfort levels.

There is little doubt that a continuous high degree of conformity at work causes some people to lose sight of themselves and to identify themselves by title, grade, status etc. If they are made redundant many of them feel that their very lives have been taken and that they have nothing to live for. This degree of identity with job and loss of self is not healthy.

Diversity and equal opportunities

One way to avoid the fear and pain of change is to give something that is already being done a new name and pretend something has changed when it hasn't. Equal opportunities has been renamed diversity and nothing has changed.

The concept of equal opportunities can be represented by Figure 5.2. Each is a human being equal to (and the same as) each other. The two apparently different people (the black circle and the misshapen circle) are said to be equal to and have the same rights as the others, but they appear different from the majority. The majority may be very different from each other, but

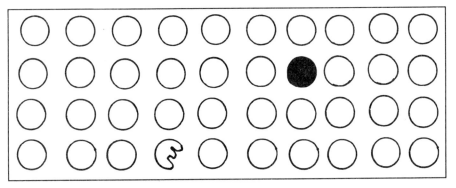

Figure 5.2   Equal opportunities

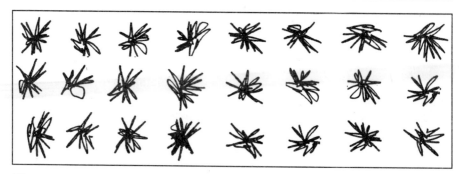

Figure 5.3   Diversity

this is hidden by the pretence that they are the same.

Diversity on the other hand is represented by Figure 5.3, where everyone is different and accepted and embraced for being different. Differences in appearance are just another difference and far less noticeable because they are welcome in an environment where any and all differences are welcome. This is diversity.

Embracing diversity as a means to improved performance does not mean establishing equal opportunity practices to legislate against discrimination. *It means welcoming discrimination so that we are all seen to be and experienced as being different.*

Personal boundaries

The spiky diagram in Figure 5.4 depicts the impact of both self-imposed and externally imposed boundaries on limiting people. The larger circle

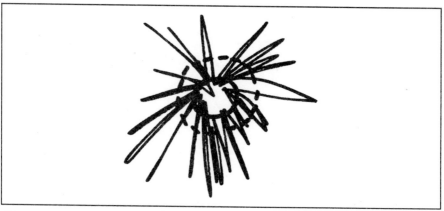

Figure 5.4   Personal boundaries

represents the individual's own boundary of how they present themselves to the world. The smaller circle is the boundary imposed by the organization they work for.

It is a common practice for organizations to produce job descriptions aimed at defining their needs. This is usually intended as a helpful device for clarifying people's roles. The modern approach is to specify these in term of required competencies. The result is to construct a *bounded* demand (shown by the inner circle on the diagram) on the people which locks out many of their capabilities so that they are once again limited.

Of course, boundaries are an essential way for us to survive in the world. We all have to decide how revealing we want and need to be. This is a form of self-protection. It is also important that we respect other people's boundaries. Sexual harassment is clearly a failure to respect boundaries.

So boundaries both contain and limit us. We need them and yet we can allow them to limit us especially if we just accept those placed on us by others. We need to find a balance between over and under exposure.

I am coming to the belief that most organizations fear the power that they will release if they remove these limits and invite people to be themselves. If organizations can find the courage to embrace individual uniqueness, with all the jagged edges, then real high performance becomes possible. The process is not an easy one. It calls for an enlightened approach to management based on *trust, freedom* and *responsibility* (see Chapter 17).

Releasing human potential

Moving from a culture of sameness (including uniforms and dress codes) to a culture of diversity is a massive leap, probably one that is too great to be accepted by most organizations, even the most adventurous.

Such a move requires commitment and hard work and, to do it successfully requires:

- guides who are supported by the chief executive and are trusted, free to act and responsible for the outcomes
- a philosophy of encouraging, welcoming, embracing and supporting differences in the form of inviting people to be their unique selves
- a balanced approach that whilst encouraging difference, does not see sameness as bad or negative, but as something that is needed for people to work together.

With these three requirements in place it is possible to establish individual performance outcomes in terms of responsibilities and to give people the freedom to use all their unique powers to fulfil these responsibilities in ways that 'suit them best' – of course, within the minimum of agreed boundaries.

Extensive rule books and procedure manuals are the tools used by authoritarian régimes to control and limit people and so reduce their performance. In the new culture these will be replaced by 'operating guidelines' that welcome initiative, encourage flexibility and pay homage to common sense.

A group of people working on the subject of diversity decided to look at themselves as a group to see in what ways they were conforming or differentiating themselves. They noticed a tendency to be gently testing boundaries and experimenting by conforming with the emerging process of working together. There was some challenging of opinions and ideas and some differentiation, but it seemed they were seeking comfort in the group's confusion about diversity. They examined the basic question of diversity and what 'it' is, its existence; how to 'see' it, recognize and reward it. Perhaps it always exists beneath the surface (inside the boundary) of the individual's conforming behaviour.

Diversity, the group decided, was what people do and how they do it. And not who they are, though that might well influence their choice about exhibiting their difference. By looking at diversity as part of a continuum of how people react to each other and their environment, conforming at one moment and differentiating themselves at another, they began to see a glimmer of clarity through the remnants of their cloud of confusion.

To open up channels of energy and to push our own and other people's boundaries demands that we acknowledge and accept our differences. From this base it is possible to grow and expand as people with all our spikiness and perform at the very pinnacle and outer limits of ourselves.

6   Helping people to perform

One of the factors of performance which can have a very significant effect on the levels achieved is the provision of relevant conditions. This is mostly, but not exclusively, the concern of managers and this chapter will focus on six key aspects of how managers can help their people to perform. The six key aspects are:

- supporting learning
- experience and practice
- challenging your people
- non-critical feedback
- power
- recognition and motivation.

Supporting learning

When people are learning they are often hesitant and unsure of their actions. In the early stages of learning they will probably hold back from 'having a go' because they are concerned that they will not be able to do it properly. This holding back from experiment and experience can considerably slow down their learning progress. If, at the exact moment of decision, you can encourage them to try and if you are able to show them that getting it wrong will not matter because you can easily put it right, you will be instrumental in helping them to learn.

Encouragement is showing people that you have confidence in them and that you trust them to do the best they can. In this atmosphere you can help them to learn quickly by using what they know or think they know. Encouragement has three elements:

- an expression of your belief that the other person can do it
- support for the person through guidance and availability
- patience and non-critical responses to 'miss-takes'.

Belief in others   Your belief in other people's ability to do something if repeated often enough, and if supported by success in small steps, will lead to their increasing self-belief. Self-belief and self-esteem are important ingredients in people having confidence to do all the learning that success requires.

Guidance and availability   You cannot encourage someone if you are not there. On the other hand you can overdo it by being a constant presence leaning over someone's shoulder as they try to perform. Find a happy balance where you can offer guidance and be available if needed.

Patience and non-critical responses   People will make 'miss-takes' when they are learning. Your patience will undoubtedly be tested over and over again as you help your people to perform. It can be hard to maintain a flow of non-critical feedback, yet this is exactly what you should do to provide an encouraging atmosphere.

Helping people to use what they have learned

When you are helping someone to learn it is very hard to watch them struggle and to remember that what matters most is the effort they make and not the outcome. In the performance cycle the focus is very much on outcomes and results. However, if the focus is only on outcomes when people are learning, it will hold back the risk that they are prepared to take. The old adage that 'it is better to try and fail than never to have tried', has been changed to 'it is better not to try if you think you might fail'. This results in a considerable slowing down of the learning progress.

If people are not encouraged to use the knowledge they have learned they will gradually lose the knowledge.

Helping people to be successful

One of my favourite sayings is 'Failures are the stepping stones to success'. Of course this is only true if people have the courage to risk failing until they succeed. Not many of us have such courage and if the result of failure is criticism and ridicule it is no wonder that we want to avoid failing.

It is possible to help people to learn and to experience being successful at the same time as they are learning, by setting up learning opportunities that they can succeed at. Computer games are a very good example of how people are offered different levels of difficulty that they can play, starting with a fairly easy level that they can succeed at. The game designers know that if players can't succeed early on they will abandon the game.

When people succeed at some new task for the first time the sense of personal achievement is considerable. The joy we all have when we discover new abilities and new powers is a tremendous boost to our spirits to go on learning and developing our skills. And it doesn't stop when we reach competency in one particular skill.

Experience and practice

Practice and experience are very different elements of our learning and development. They are sometimes confused with each other. I once interviewed an applicant for a job by asking her about her experience in designing training programmes. She answered that she had fifteen years' experience of designing training programmes. When I looked more closely at what she had been doing the reality was that she had one year's experience repeated fifteen times. She was very 'practised' at designing a particular kind of training programme for technical staff in a single company. Her 'experience' was very limited. Here are my definitions for practice and experience.

Practice   The repeated performance of a task so that its future performance becomes embedded or ingrained in the performer's behaviour thus enabling it to be carried out time and time again in exactly the same way.

Experience   Participation in a wide variety of events and situations which results in the enhancement of learning and brings clarity of understanding to the application of existing knowledge and skills and/or the acquisition of new knowledge and skills.

Some years ago I decided to learn to play golf. I bought some clubs. I had some lessons and I started to play with a friend who was a much more experienced golfer. After a few rounds at which I performed terribly I had some more lessons. My teacher suggested that I bought 100 secondhand golf balls and that I practised once a week hitting them down the practice field with my driver, then back up the field with an iron, then down the field with my pitching wedge. Then go on the putting green and putt until I was tired. He suggested that I did this on Wednesday and then play a round of golf on Friday. I practised this for a couple of weeks and started to play a reasonable round of golf.

For various reasons my practising became less and less until I stopped

altogether. My experience playing different golf courses increased, as did my experience of a wide variety of rough areas, woodland, sand traps, streams, rivers and lakes bordering and strategically located on the various golf courses I played. My golf stayed about the same, terrible.

I have now decided not to play golf. I do not have the motivation to practise so I do not get any pleasure out of my experience of playing golf. I am sure that if I was prepared to practise until I reached a certain satisfactory level of performance that I could then relax a little and enjoy my experience. I am simply not prepared to put in that much effort practising.

Recognising the elements of experience

Experience has four elements:

- something new that I have never met before
- something that seems similar but is different
- something which involves my participation
- something which is challenging and involves some risk.

Facing the new requires people to call upon their reserves of knowledge and skills and to find some personal resource to deal with the situation. The new is often risky and challenging simply because it is new. People often discover that they can handle this new situation and in the process they tap into aspects of themselves that they may have been unaware they had.

The similar but different situation can be difficult to handle because the initial response is to call on the previous experience to which this one is similar as a way of deciding what to do. Because this situation is different people find that they have to adapt the previous response in order to deal with the current event and so enhance their learning.

Participation is a crucial part of experience. People have to be involved in what is happening. Deciding what to do and how to do it is part of the learning that comes with experience. If you stand back and observe others you have not experienced the event. You have to be part of something to experience it.

Challenging and risky situations call for more than the application of knowledge and skill. The more experience people have had the more likely they are to be confident to attempt challenging and risky situations. They must be willing to 'have a go' and, possibly, to fail. If people are scared of failing and if the environment is not tolerant of failure people are unlikely to take the risk. This consequently limits their experience. It is very important for people to learn that they can survive failure.

You can see that experience is very different from practice. So the expression, 'she is a practised manager' means something quite different from, 'she is an experienced manager'.

Experiencing is learning not mastering

If you want to master something you have to focus your attention on what it is you want to master and you have to practise and practise until you have mastered it. Your experience is thus limited to the task you want to master. You may seek experience in using the skill you are mastering, but this will be in a narrow area of the skill itself.

Experiencing, on the other hand, is a process of learning and extending your horizons. It calls on the whole of your organismic learning power, your physical, psychological and spiritual capabilities and values. You have to bring everything you are to the experience.

Experience is a test of what you know and can do. It requires you to explore the experience to discover things that you are not already aware of. You experiment with new ways of doing things, new attitudes and new ideas. Experience is about change, a willingness to adapt, to be different.

Practice alone will never equip anyone to deal with all the eventualities that are likely to arise in their lives, and experience without practice will probably be at best unenjoyable (as my golf was) and at worst quite frightening.

Helping people to perform means encouraging them to be open to change, to experience more and to be willing to explore their own potential.

Practice makes perfect

It has long been held that the more we practise something the better we become. But whether we learn from practice or practise what we learn is quite another question.

I have three juggling balls and from time to time I juggle them for a few minutes. Whenever I pick them up I can start juggling immediately. When I first learned to juggle I was shown how to do it, i.e. someone demonstrated the skill to me. I was then encouraged to juggle two balls with one hand and then to introduce the third ball. I gradually learned how to juggle. Once I had the idea of what to do and my hands and eyes became coordinated I could practise. By practising I can now juggle three balls. No matter how much more I practise it will not help me to juggle four balls until I learn how to do it.

In order to practise I have to keep repeating the task over and over again.

Each time I do this my mind and body make very tiny adjustments, or corrections, so that I slowly get better at what I am doing. Eventually the task becomes ingrained in my muscles and embedded in my mind. I can do it automatically.

So in the sense of being able to repeat a task to a high level of competence practice does make perfect. By repeating the task time and time again, or drilling ourselves, we can become conditioned to perform instinctively. The legendary gunfighters of the American West became lightning fast on the draw and accurate by this process of continuous drill. It is a method used for training soldiers to respond automatically and to a high level of competence under extreme conditions.

But change the conditions and what happens?

In my juggling if I were to change the soft balls for crystal goblets or knives I am pretty sure I wouldn't be able to juggle them. I could learn if the conditions were to be accepting of my mistakes. If it didn't matter how many goblets I broke, or if I could protect my hands from being cut by the knives, then I could make the corrections that each mistake would signal were necessary.

So practice is really the art of making mistakes. Each mistake feeds a signal back to the body and the mind and a small correction is made for the next attempt. Can you recall learning to ride a bicycle? The very wobbly first attempt became honed through the corrections signalled by many mistakes to a confident smooth ride.

If people are expected to practise in an environment that is intolerant of mistakes it will be very difficult for them to have the freedom necessary to rapidly increase their skills. The fear of failure stops people from practising.

Practice can also be boring and so people need to be encouraged and motivated to practice. I gave up golf because of my lack of interest and my boredom with practising, and I had little encouragement from anyone else to help me to continue.

Learning from mistakes

Mistakes are an opportunity to learn. Of course this is only true if the people making the mistakes are aware of the learning they can do and if the manager recognizes the mistake as an opportunity to learn rather than as a nuisance, or as a reason for criticism and discipline.

The response of someone who is criticized in a negative way is rarely positive, but 'constructive criticism' is a contradiction in terms. The opposite of negative criticism is positive feedback, which involves no criticism at all.

So how can we help people to learn from mistakes? First, we can think of mistakes as 'miss-takes'. In the film industry even the best and most skilled actors have many 'takes' in order to get a sequence just right. There is no criticism. Instead there is encouragement and suggestion from the director which the best actors respond to and learn from. That is how they become the best.

A 'miss-take' then is a chance to learn, but learning will not happen unless the person making the 'miss-take' is able to see what might be changed in order to make the next attempt a 'good-take'.

When people make 'miss-takes' managers might find the following four suggestions helpful:

- acknowledge the 'miss-take' non-critically (see Chapter 11)
- find out from them what happened (awareness)
- show them what to do
- ask them to demonstrate that they can do it.

Awareness of what is happening is crucial to making changes in carrying out the task, and it is the performer's awareness which needs to be focused on. Telling people what you think is happening is not enough unless they know what they are doing and how they could change.

Stay with this cycle of activity until they are happy that they can do it in the required way – this is 'guided practice' in action.

Removing the fear of failure

In the minds of many mistakes are synonymous with failure, and failure means criticism, ridicule and even punishment. This results in people developing a poor opinion of themselves and losing confidence – little wonder that many people fear failure. To remove this fear people need to be able to learn in an atmosphere that completely rejects any idea of failure, an atmosphere where mistakes are:

- treated as 'miss-takes'
- never criticized
- never punished
- seen as a chance to learn
- seen as stepping stones to success.

In this way mistakes are not seen as failures, but as a positive result of practice towards becoming successful.

Challenging your people

Throwing people in at the deep end is one way of challenging them, it is also a good way of 'killing them off', metaphorically speaking of course. There are three other less risky and more supportive ways of challenging your people:

- keeping them on their toes
- inviting people to grow
- sharing your job.

Keeping them on their toes

I am not sure if this saying comes from ballet, or whether it simply means standing on tiptoe to reach for something. Either way you can imagine how challenging it would be to stay on your toes for a long time. The saying has come to mean keeping people constantly focused on what they are doing and getting them to reach beyond themselves.

In terms of helping people to perform it is to be aware of when they can perform comfortably and to find additional tasks that will stretch them further. This is one way to rise from the plateau of competency to the summit of high performance.

Inviting people to grow

Here are four questions that you could ask your staff. They are all invitations to grow.

- Would you like a change from what you are doing?
- Are you interested in doing ...?
- Would you like to help me with ...?
- There are several additional tasks I would like you to do. Which would you prefer?

Stop for a moment and imagine how you would feel if your manager were to ask you one of these questions. You might feel excited, apprehensive, suspicious, depending on your relationship with your manager, but you would be stirred in some way.

If the questions contain some interesting and stretching activity they become a form of confirmation of the person's ability. Think about each member of your staff and see if you can find a way of inviting them to grow.

Sharing your job

Some aspects of your job would probably make excellent learning opportunities for your staff. If you invite people to take on part of what you do you should consider providing support for them whilst they are doing it. Consider the following opportunities:

- Invite a member of your staff to do your job for one day.
- Ask one of your staff to accompany you to a meeting.
- Invite someone to attend a meeting in your place.
- Select a particular task you have to do and invite one of your staff to do it.

You can probably think of other ways to give your staff challenging opportunities by sharing your job. Remember the following advice:

- Brief the person concerned.
- Be available to help them.
- Encourage them.
- Don't criticize them if they make a 'miss-take'.

Perhaps the overall key to providing work-based learning opportunities is to use real activities, or create simulations which are close to reality. When your staff do this with your help and support it can lead to significant increases in competence, confidence and performance.

Non-critical feedback

Put this book down for a moment and think back to when you were last criticized. Picture the scene in your mind. See the face of the person criticizing you and hear the words again. Note how you are feeling and the thoughts that drift through your mind as you hear the criticism.

I doubt if you enjoy remembering the experience. I cannot know how you feel when you are criticized. I usually feel angry, annoyed, belittled, and I try to deal with these feelings by seeing what I can learn from the experience, but I never enjoy criticism.

In giving positive feedback the aim is to be accurate in what you have to say and yet give the recipient a sense of comfort so that they fully hear what you are saying without letting their feelings interrupt their listening.

The skills of giving positive feedback include:

- giving praise
- encouraging people
- knowing how to avoid being patronizing
- knowing how to dwell on the positive.

Giving praise

Praise is a gift that we are unwilling to give yet long to receive. Perhaps this is because we are not attuned to looking for the good, to admire strength, but to searching out fault and weakness.

> People ask you for criticism, but they only want praise.
>
> Somerset Maugham[1]

To give praise effectively you need to:

- recognise that something has been done to warrant praise
- respond immediately
- use simple words
- be precise and neither understate or overstate your appreciation.

For example:

> I noticed how well you handled that complaint and I want you to know that I appreciated your clarity and the way you were sympathetic and yet firm with the customer.

When praise is given in this straightforward way it confirms the person's actions and reinforces their learning and experience. If praise is overstated it has the opposite effect. Most of us are aware of how well we are performing and whether or not we deserve praise. So to receive it when we don't think we deserve it immediately changes it, in our minds, into sarcasm. Praise is a very important part of the process of helping people to learn, and it has to be handled carefully and appropriately.

> There is no such whetstone, to sharpen a good wit and encourage a will to learning, as is praise.
>
> Roger Ascham[2]

Avoiding being patronizing

There is a tendency when giving feedback, especially praise, to sound condescending and patronizing. This happens when we use language which tends to make us sound parental and judgemental. For example:

> I am very pleased with you for ...
> I think you are working well.
> I'm glad you've been able to grasp ...
> I'm very satisfied with you.

The problem is partly in the words we choose and partly in how we use and deliver them. The way to avoid being patronizing is to state what is happening and what you think about the work rather than the person. By concentrating on the work itself you avoid making any judgement about the person. For example:

> I like the way that you spoke to Mrs Smith and listened to her reply. You could probably tell from her response that you dealt with her complaint very well. It was a good piece of work.

By focusing on the work and the person's performance it is possible to be clear and direct without the risk of sounding patronizing or condescending.

Dwelling on the positive

Good positive feedback is often spoilt by the tendency that some people have to sneak in a negative comment as an afterthought. For example:

> I like the way that you spoke to Mrs Smith and listened to her reply. You could probably tell from her response that you dealt with her complaint very well. It was a good piece of work. It would be nice if you could do it more often.

Another way of spoiling good feedback is by using the word 'but' to introduce a negative point. For example:

> The way you close sales is excellent and your success ratio is very high, but your after sales support leaves a lot to be desired.

The opening positive comment is completely overtaken by the final sneaky negative comment. It is important when giving feedback to separate the praiseworthy from the problematic, so that each receives the appropriate focus and emphasis.

Avoiding negative feedback

Whether or not you choose to give negative feedback is entirely up to you. It can have the effect of motivating people to perform. To tell people that they can't do something may well motivate them to prove you are wrong. However, I have found that negative feedback tends to demotivate people. If they are told something often enough they come to believe it.

It is easy to avoid negative feedback by being simple, direct and non-critical. You can deal with almost any situation in a positive way by looking at what you want to happen rather than dwelling on what has happened, and by looking at the activity and not the person.

Imagine what you would say to a member of your staff who has avoided doing something you have asked them to do. You have reminded them several times and still they have not done what you want. Think for a moment how you would feel, then think about how you would tackle them.

Here is an approach you might take:

Be simple and state the obvious   'I have asked you several times to do ... and you have not done it yet. What's going on?'

Listen to the answer without commenting   'I'm sorry but I don't want to do it because it's something that one of the junior staff should do.'

Be direct and say what you feel   'I find your approach to avoiding doing what I asked quite frustrating and I wished that you had told me earlier about the problem you are having. Now what are we going to do about it?'

Agree a solution   'I would like you to ask someone junior to me to do it.'
'Well I didn't do that because everyone is so busy. OK, I tell you what, I'll do it and we'll just forget that I asked you.'
'No, it's OK. I didn't realize we were so busy. I'll do it.'
'Are you sure?'
'Yes, I'm sure.'
'OK, good. Thanks.'

This example could have gone a number of ways, but whichever way the manager could still have kept the feedback positive. The alternative might have been to get into some kind of power or status argument which undoubtedly would have become negative.

There are two other important aspects of keeping feedback positive:

● deliberately using criticism as a weapon
● projecting our own feelings onto others.

Deliberately using criticism

We can, and much to our discredit, we do use criticism to hurt and wound others. Our need to do this is in some measure determined by how we ourselves have been subjected to criticism in our past. That we do it at all is much to be regretted and it can always be avoided no matter how significant the provocation.

Using criticism in this way is our last defence and a rather mean one at that. We can see no way of dealing with the matter more positively, or we choose not to. Criticism is, in effect, a failure to find a more appropriate way of dealing with the issue. When we criticize in a negative way we diminish the person we criticize and we diminish ourselves for having to resort to criticism. What people call constructive criticism is in fact positive feedback.

Projecting our own feelings onto others

If I say to someone, 'You frustrate me', I am in fact saying, 'I am frustrated'. Rather than own and be responsible for how I am feeling, I blame the other person. This is a common occurrence especially in an organizational setting. There are many situations in which people are criticized and blamed for the feelings their managers are having.

When a difficulty arises it usually generates feelings between the people involved. These feelings can get in the way of finding a solution, especially if each person is projecting their feelings onto the other.

There is a straightforward four-step approach to dealing with this situation:

Step 1   State what happens: 'When you do ...'
Step 2   State how you feel: 'I feel ...'
Step 3   State why: 'Because ...'
Step 4   State what you want: 'I would prefer it if you ...'

Here is an example of two people who are using the four step approach.

> When you don't arrive on time I feel angry because I have to fill in for you. I would prefer it if you were here on time or let me know you are going to be late.

> When you shout at me because I am late I feel upset because you don't know about my problems getting Jimmy to school. I would prefer it if we could agree for me to start half an hour later.

This form of communication is very powerful because it is open and honest. Feelings are owned instead of projected and each person's point of view is heard by the other. It is a simple formula for dealing with most relationship difficulties in the workplace and you will notice that it is totally positive feedback.

Openness and honesty

One of the problems of giving good positive feedback is not to leave anything unsaid. This is much more difficult to do than to say. (Imagine the problems that might arise if you were to speak your thoughts without censoring them.) However, what I mean is saying what you want to say. Here is a short conversation where neither person is saying what they want to say:

Mary	Oh heavens, it's raining and I have to walk home tonight.
Joan	I can give you a lift if you want.
Mary	No, it's all right really. The walk will do me good.
Joan	Are you sure.
Mary	Yes, honestly.

The outcome is that Mary walks home and gets sopping wet and is annoyed that Joan didn't give her a lift. Joan feels guilty for not taking Mary, but blames her for insisting that she didn't need a lift. Here is the revised version:

Mary	Oh heavens, it's raining. Could you give me a lift?
Joan	Well, it's a bit out of my way, but seeing as it's raining ...
Mary	Thanks, I appreciate it. Perhaps I can return the favour sometime?
Joan	OK, I'll hold you to that.

By being open and direct people often feel that it leaves them exposed. It offers few escape paths of the 'I didn't really mean that' or the 'Why didn't you say?' variety. You have to 'come clean' and this can make you feel vulnerable to a less open person.

Giving feedback is all about saying it as it is, focusing on the positive and leaving people feeling better informed and feeling better.

Power

Most people are able to exercise two levels of power – personal power and role power, and for some there is a third level – reflected power.

Personal power is associated with confidence and self-esteem and enables people to make choices and decisions in a way that ensures they live as they want to.

People with a strong sense of personal power are able to listen to the ideas and suggestions of others, to weigh up the advice they receive, and then act to suit themselves without being unduly swayed in the direction others might want them to be.

Role power is the power people have because of the role they are exercising at the time. It is possible to have several roles each of which carries a certain power. For example, you could be a father or mother, a manager, a husband or wife, captain of the hockey team, and so on. In each of these roles there is a certain designated (assumed) power. It might be specified by the organization for whom we play the role, or implied from our experience or the expectations of others.

Reflected power is a level of power exercised by those close to 'powerful' people. They bask in the power that emanates from their more powerful companions. Personal assistants often operate with the reflected role power of their bosses. Children can express the reflected power of their parents – being the son of a prime minister, for example, can carry with it a lot of reflected power. Husbands and wives often operate with the reflected power of their partners.

This reflected power may be mistaken as the personal or role power of the individuals themselves, rather than the person they are close to. The problem with this is the loss of sight as to whose power is being exercised. Recognizing and using reflected power is a valuable attribute. It needs full awareness on the part of the people using it.

In exercising power we all operate with a combination of personal power and role power and sometimes reflected power. The extent to which we are able to fully utilize our power depends on factors such as our upbringing, education, training, experience, our roles, the people around us, and so on.

Getting people to own their power

If people have 'personal power' and 'role power', how do they disempower themselves? Here are a few clues:

- When they exercise power they have to take responsibility for what they do.
- When they make choices they have to live with the consequences.
- When they use their power other people criticize and blame them for what happens.
- Exercising power can be scary.

Many people find life more comfortable and have an artificial sense of security if others exercise power on their behalf. They are, in fact, giving away their power and unfortunately there are plenty of others who are willing to take it from them. I say unfortunately because, in effect, those who take the power only receive it by dint of their role. This forsaken power can in no way enhance the recipients' personal power which is evidenced when they leave the role.

Here are some of the ways that people give away their power:

- What would you do?
- I just can't do it. Would you do it, please?
- It's really up to you.
- You're the Chair.
- I don't have a choice.
- If that's what you think, I'd better do it?
- What do you want me to do about ...?

In each case you can refuse to take their power by getting them to act for themselves. Can you think of ways of dealing with each of the examples above?

Not giving people your power

As others may give away their power so might you. Even if you are aware of the possibility of giving away your power, you can still do so.

The important thing to be clear about is: Whose power are you exercising?

It is very helpful to clearly separate out your personal power and your role power and any reflected power that you might be exercising. This will answer the question about whose power it is. If you are ever in doubt, stop and consider what is happening and decide who should be exercising power over events.

Of course there will be moments when people are competing for power, but remember they can only compete for role power. Your personal power is yours, unless you give it away. I have always been interested in the question: Do leaders lead because followers follow? Or vice versa?

Not taking other people's power

There is a great temptation to take someone else's power when they offer it to us. There is an immediate feeling of superiority and our ego gains a significant boost. It is possible to fall into this trap even if you don't want to take the power. The trainer who stands in front of an audience is often the recipient of the power of the audience. Some trainers enjoy this sense of power and talk about the 'buzz' they get from training. The frustration of teenagers at school has a lot to do with their newly discovered personal power being taken from them temporarily by teachers.

Some managers take the power of their staff and bask in their feelings of self-importance. Politicians deliberately take the power of the people through public oratory. They then exercise the power of the people on behalf of the people. Far too many politicians forget whose power it is and act as if it is their own.

You can avoid taking other people's power by acting in three ways:

- Recognize when people are deliberately or unintentionally declining to use their own power.
- Be aware of the extent of your own personal and role power and any reflected power that you might use.
- Refuse to exercise anyone else's power.

The question of maintaining power boundaries is fundamental to empowerment and performance. If we see empowerment as the process by which people take power then it has three components:

- realization and acceptance of personal power
- investment of power in the role being carried out
- the extent to which access is available to reflected power.

These three components determine the power boundaries.

Recognition and motivation

People like to be 'seen' and appreciated for what they do. It is in fact a fundamental human need and the basis of self-esteem and self-confidence. You will help your people to perform as much by recognizing their achievements as by the very best of coaching and support.

Recognition makes people feel special. They feel noticed and therefore important in that moment. This feeds messages of acceptance, acknowledgement and respect into their psyche and directly boosts their self-esteem and self-confidence. The effects are powerful motivating factors for the future.

You should take every opportunity, no matter how small it might seem, to recognize what your people are doing.

Motivating people

Motivation is something that we recognize in ourselves when we are keen to do something. Recognizing it and creating it in others is quite different. What is motivation? Here are some definitions:

The Oxford English Dictionary   The act of moving or inducing a person to act in a certain way; a desire, fear, reason, etc. which influences a person's volition.

The Universal Dictionary   The mental process, function, or instinct that produces and sustains incentive or drive in human and animal behaviour.

Both these definitions imply that motivation is some kind of force or power that determines the way people act. Neither attempts to state where the force comes from. I believe that motivation is the fire that burns within everyone. It is there all the time and is fuelled by people's past experience and the conditioning they have had in their lives. It is stimulated by their thoughts and by external events that occur in their personal environment. My definition of motivation is:

> The inner force that makes each person pursue courses of action, both positive and negative, which lead to the satisfaction of some personal desire.

In helping your people to be motivated to high levels of performance you need to be able to help them to tap into their own inner force.

In addition it is helpful to identify what motivates your people to achieve high levels of performance. You will probably find that recognition, respect and reward feature prominently on the agenda.

References

1   Maugham, W. Somerset, *Of Human Bondage*, Mandarin, London, 1990.
2   Ascham, Roger, *The Schoolmaster*, Thoemmes Press, Bristol, 1994.

Part 2

Performance management

7 The performance management cycle

A continuous process

Working and performing is part of a continuous life-cycle that ebbs and flows and which always moves forwards. As we travel along this life-cycle, and as we learn from our experience, the way we travel changes. We apply what we have learnt to our present activity so that we influence the future outcomes of this activity.

People are self-regulating organisms constantly searching for satisfying fulfilment of what they are doing. This natural process will pressure people into trying to reach completion. The performance cycle describes one view of how we do this and can be represented as a wave (see Figure 7.1). The crest of the wave being our action and performance and the troughs being time for reflection and learning.

This performance cycle takes place as a natural process when we perform. However, it does not always flow smoothly. It is possible, and an almost inevitable consequence of the way we function as human beings, that the cycle will be interrupted.

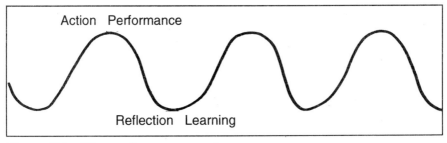

Figure 7.1   The performance cycle wave

Interrupting the performance cycle

It is an all too frequent occurrence for both managers and performers to interrupt the performance cycle. This may be conscious or unconscious behaviour. The main reason for interrupting the cycle is the inherent desire we all have to protect ourselves and to survive in the world.

In order to survive, right from the beginning of our lives, we learn and develop ways of being that bring us what we need. You only have to watch a newborn baby to see the process at work. This tiny human being is completely, organismically, self-regulating, demanding food and sleep and basic hygiene exactly when it needs it. As time passes the baby learns what works and what doesn't work in its particular environment and adapts accordingly.

Eventually this learning takes on the messages from parents, teachers and others who care for and influence the growing child. These messages begin to 'condition' the way we are. Here are a few you will know:

Children should be seen and not heard.
Little boys don't cry.
Little girls don't fight.

There are thousands of these messages – many much harsher and more damaging to the developing person – but we learn how to survive in spite of what we hear and how we are treated. We develop ways of 'blocking' our natural process flow to fit into the unnatural demands placed on us.

As we grow older we realize that to feel 'safe', i.e. acceptable and loved, we have to fit into a particular pattern of behaviour that suits our care takers. So we do what is necessary and we block our natural process to scream when we are mad, to hit someone when they hit us, to cry when we are hurt, to scream with pleasure, to throw jelly around, to make a mess, and so on.

When we enter the world of work we continue this blocking process as we learn what is 'expected' behaviour in this new environment. We dress 'appropriately' and behave in 'acceptable' ways. We need to belong, to be accepted and to be loved so we block our natural individuality, our natural process in order to survive and protect ourselves.

After many years of developing such survival strategies we can become 'stuck' in habitual ways of being that might not satisfy us. These habitual ways of interrupting our contact with our environment and other people have grown as a form of protection and in protecting us they can impede our contact, prevent us completing our interactions and interrupt our performance. In other words we become expert blockers of our own natural process, and we do it in a wide variety of ways.

Ways of interrupting our process flow

Switching off our senses, not seeing, not hearing etc., can be a very effective way of protecting ourselves. I have spent much of my life wearing a very strong suit of armour. I felt protected and at the same time I couldn't feel the world outside. Desensitizing ourselves is a very powerful way of avoiding being hurt. Sometimes as a 'man of action' I have blundered over other people's opinions and smashed down legitimate and valuable objections to what I was doing.

Casting off what we don't want to hear or feel is another effective form of protection – with my armour went a very large shield which has until recently served me very well, deflecting missiles of all shapes and sizes. It has also stopped me receiving many of the things I wanted to see, hear and feel. I can recall times when I saw all praise as flattery and ignored it in the belief that the flatterers wanted something from me.

Taking in when it is done without being selective, i.e. when the messages are gulped down and obeyed without thinking, actually stops me from rejecting what I don't want. Like overeating, I feel full and sick and I want to spit out. And yet I do need to take in the information that is useful and I need to be selective about it. I have often taken in the 'shoulds' of my bosses, trying to please them and refusing to follow my own instincts, often to my cost.

Putting out our own ideas as if they are someone else's. Disowning what we believe and projecting it onto others can be unreal and unauthentic. 'You shouldn't interrupt people' is a projection – what I really mean is 'I don't like being interrupted'. With my armour and shield goes a large sharp sword which has also served me well.

Going inside where I feel safe and protected is useful and I try to make sure that I don't do to myself what I want to do to others; that when I am angry with someone else I am not angry instead with myself, or when I want to hurt someone else that I don't hurt myself. I can remember times when I used to 'take my bat home' when something wasn't how I wanted it – 'cutting off my nose to spite my face'.

Merging with others because I need to belong can lead to me losing myself. When I merge, or become confluent, I lose sight of me and my needs and focus only on others, which means that my needs are not met. Conforming is a protective and helpful way to operate, and at the same time I am aware of my own uniqueness. Sometimes it's easier to agree than to stick your neck out, but it rarely improves performance.

These ways of interrupting our natural process flow are also useful to protect ourselves and keep ourselves intact. We need to be aware of how to use them in a way that best serves our needs and helps us to perform successfully and reach satisfaction.

Restoring process flow

The first thing I need to do is to honour myself. I am a unique individual. I owe it to myself to be as real as I can in my contact with others. I see organizations as relationship systems where people function mainly through their interactions with other people. If these interactions are not effective, then neither is the organization. For relationships to be effective people have to honour themselves and be real.

We need to listen to what we need – listen to our own thoughts and ideas, and listen to others so that we can take in what we want and spit out what we don't want. By doing this we can become aware of what is going on for us at this moment. Then we can choose what to do.

I have laid down my sword and shield and I have climbed out of my armour. They are still available if I should ever need them. In the meantime I am more real, more present and more aware of who I am and I perform better than ever.

Allowing people to achieve

When studies have been done to discover what people want from work, time and again a 'sense of achievement' comes out on or near the top of the list. A sense of achievement is only possible if people recognize that they have had to push themselves. In other words, they perform at a level above their own expectations of themselves.

It is important for people to experience success, to enjoy the recognition and applause that go with it. People have to have an inner belief that they can do what they are being asked to do, even if they recognize that it is something better than they have ever done before. Such outcomes and results bring a strong sense of achievement and the heady feelings of success. The pleasure of success has three very important effects. First, it boosts self-esteem; second, it increases self-confidence, and third, it encourages further development/learning.

As time passes and people grow the goalposts will move. It becomes easy to perform at previously unattainable levels and the sense of achievement and success decline. There is nothing wrong with moving the goalposts, in fact it is necessary to maintain interest and excitement. The key is to move them by small steps at a time and in agreement with the people concerned.

Mutually agreed outcomes and results are a much better incentive than targets which are set by someone else. And sometimes people want to aim for far higher levels than managers might have set for them. Of course there are always those who will be looking for the easy option and managers can push them to their limits. Even so, if the outcomes and results are not mutually agreed people are unlikely to be committed to them.

When people are invited to be part of the performance management process and to increase their awareness about what is needed, paying attention to their own development, acting appropriately, participating in reviewing and coaching and finally reflecting, learning and enjoying their success, performance is certain to improve.

The analogy of the wave lends itself to this process of performance management (see Figure 7.2).

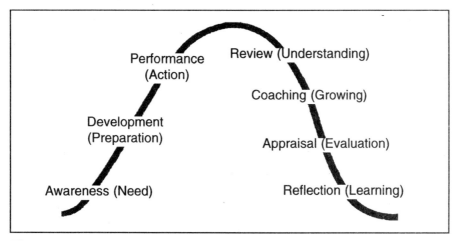

Figure 7.2   The stages of performance management

Awareness

The awareness phase is not really the start because it follows reflection at the end of the previous wave and is a 'new' awareness of needs that have to be met to complete the next cycle. In the awareness phase plans are made for the desired levels of performance. It is, in effect, the planning process of the cycle and it contains three elements:

- specific outputs in the form of outcomes and results
- explicit ways in which the five 'performance factors' will be addressed
- boundaries in terms of responsibilities.

These three elements together represent what is expected of the person concerned. (See Chapter 8 for a full explanation of the awareness stage of the cycle.)

Development

The development phase focuses on how we can prepare, get ready and equip ourselves for the performance that is expected of us. In the awareness stage we try to be explicit about the way that the 'five performance factors' will be addressed. In the development stage we take this further and actually prepare and equip ourselves so that we are able to perform to the best of our abilities. (See Chapter 9 for a full discussion of this stage of the cycle.)

Performance

The performance phase is the time when we use all of 'what we bring' to take action in the best possible way.

Review

The review phase helps us to understand what happened when we took action. It is the opportunity to identify what we could do differently to improve our performance in the future. This calls for continuous attention to what is happening with a sharp focus on performance. It is the stage at which we monitor how well the bridge building is going and the extent of the 'performance gap' which still needs to be spanned.

During review discussions the focus will be on what we can do to improve performance and achieve specified outcomes and results. It is far more positive and effective to focus on making improvements than on things that are being done wrong. It is important to recognize when people are having difficulties and problems in their daily work, and to deal with them when they arise. Performance review is not about having scheduled review meetings, although this might form a part of the review process. Performance review is about supporting performers *as they perform*, not waiting for something to go wrong. (See Chapter 10 for a detailed discussion on this stage of the cycle.)

Coaching

Coaching follows the review stage as a natural flow into working 'on the job' with performers to encourage them and to increase their confidence. The aim of coaching is to look for indications of good aspects of performance and to offer suggestions for improvement. When people seek to improve their performance they need feedback and encouragement to keep trying. There is no advantage in simply telling them what they are doing wrong. The important information is *what to do differently* to improve. (See Chapter 11 for an extensive coaching model.)

Perhaps the coaching phase is the place where we can experiment and explore how to be and work differently and in the process grow as performers.

Appraisal

The appraisal phase is the point at which we evaluate 'what we produce' from our performance and look at and measure the outcomes. Performance appraisal is a mixture of *measurement, assessment, recognition, success* and *satisfaction.* All too often the appraisal stage of the cycle is experienced by performers as judgemental and fault finding. Many, if not most, appraisal procedures are subjective evaluations of people and how they are 'perceived' to have performed by their immediate superiors. Many people do not look forward to their appraisal.

Appraisals should be a time for enjoying the recognition and respect of managers and peers for good performance. If performance has not been up to expectations then it should be a time for looking forward to how improvements can be made. The whole nature of appraisals should be positive and forward looking. (See Chapter 12 for a discussion of how appraisals can and should be handled.)

Reflection

This final phase of the cycle gives us the time we need to reflect on what we have learnt and how we are able to be different so that our needs for the next cycle also reflect how we have changed.

Involvement and participation

The performance management cycle invites the involvement and participation of everyone concerned. From establishing expectations to appraising success the whole cycle is one of cooperation. It entails discussion and agreement about expected outcomes and targets and, though people may feel stretched and challenged, it should provide them with a sense of involvement. In a supportive environment this is likely to lead to significantly improved performance.

A scenario of the cycle in practice

Coach	You know David, that was your best jump yet.
David	But I hit the bar.
Coach	Yes, but you were so close. I think if we concentrate on your fitness for the next two weeks, and then tidy up your technique we should be OK for the championships.
David	You mean I'll be able to clear 2.20?
Coach	I don't see why not, but let's take it a step at a time.

A few weeks later after the regional finals they were discussing progress.

Coach	So tell me what happened at the finals.
David	Well, I was going great then I just seemed to lose it.
Coach	What happened?
David	All my energy seemed to drain away, I just lost my edge.
Coach	OK, this is what I saw. You were pushing hard and seemed to put everything into the third jump at 2.15. It was a hot day, and I could see you were tiring, and I'm not surprised. It seemed to me that after the great jump at 2.15 your stamina gave out, and maybe your self-belief wavered.
David	Yeah, well that seems a pretty accurate assessment. So what now?
Coach	Right, here's how I rate your last performance – strength 9, technique 9, commitment 9, stamina 6, confidence 8, self-belief 6 – Do you agree?
David	OK, so where do we go next?
Coach	I think we need to build up your stamina, then jump a few 2.20s to build up your self-belief, because I know you can do it.

This scenario shows how the cycle is a joint approach to performance improvement. David cannot improve without the observations and feedback of his coach. They both have to be involved and participate in the process.

They both also need to be committed to David's improvement.

Performance management means managing this cycle. It means being constantly aware of what is happening, how it will affect performance and taking steps to adjust action accordingly. It is the joint responsibility of performers and their managers.

Management and performance

Performance management achieves its aims by accepting the golden rule that:

Management is the art of achieving success through others.

Imagine you are a manager responsible for a sales team. The team performs really well beating its targets for the month. But is it *your* performance? It is if you remember the golden rule of management, because you will have ensured the success of the team by ensuring the success of each individual member.

Most people do in fact perform as members of a team. For the managers of teams it is the performance of the team as a whole which determines how well the team manager performs.

The manager of a football team is an excellent example of where the manager's performance is judged by how well the team performs. The football manager has to sit on the sidelines whilst the team is performing. You will have watched matches where one team is playing badly, but when they come out for the second half their performance is transformed. What happened in the changing room? Certainly something did to explain the change. Helping others to perform well is a primary skill of good management. Of course, unlike football, business managers are more likely to be player managers, not sitting on the sidelines but working alongside their people as they perform together. *Good performance takes thought and effort – it doesn't happen by accident.*

Responsibilities for performance

Managers cannot make people perform. When the pyramids were built the slave masters used starvation and whips to make people perform. Later the Romans, far more cunning, realized that half-starved and half-dead slaves were pretty rotten performers and so they used the promise of good food and wine and other vicarious pleasures to motivate their slaves to perform.

Today the use of economic whips and emotional starvation still exists. However, more enlightened organizations recognize that people who are well rewarded and emotionally fed outperform those under the threat of economic sanction. In this enlightened environment performers and managers work together to manage performance.

Responsibilities of managers

Managers have four main responsibilities in the performance management process:

- to create the best environment and conditions
- to encourage and support the performer, which includes review and coaching
- to provide relevant, timely and non-critical feedback
- to develop and monitor procedures for ensuring the continuous flow of the performance management process.

Responsibilities of performers

Performers also have four main responsibilities in the performance management process:

- to pay attention to their personal desires, personal state and personal competencies and to focus them on the performance task
- to ask for help when they need it
- to provide feedback to managers and respond to feedback received
- to participate fully in the performance management process.

Both these sets of responsibilities can only be fully met in an atmosphere of mutual respect and cooperation.

Reinforcing ownership

One basic requirement of the performance cycle is that people own their performance. It is true that there are many factors outside the control of individuals which impact on their performance. These external factors do not change the nature of the ownership of performance. Racing cyclists who fall in rainy conditions can blame the rain and the slippy surface, but at the end of the day it is still *their* performance.

Managers and performers share responsibility for performance, but they do not share ownership. My performance is my performance. The factors which impact on my performance are the very things that I have to cope with when I perform. If these can be changed and improved so much the better and I may perform at a higher level. How I react to the factors of performance and how I improve are aspects of my attitude and commitment. I own my own performance.

Through my performance I may have an impact on my team's performance and I am responsible and own this impact. Other members of the team have to cope with the impact of my performance but they don't own it. Being clear about who owns what is an important part of linking individual performance with team performance. The continuous nature of the performance cycle should be fully understood and clearly defined in every work situation. Paying attention to what needs doing to improve cannot be done by looking at the past. It is our action in the present, at this moment, which conditions our performance in the future.

> Our deepest fear is not that we are inadequate but that we are powerful beyond measure. It is our light, not our darkness that most frightens us. We ask ourselves 'Who am I to be brilliant, talented, famous?' Actually who are you not to be? As we let our light shine we give others permission to do the same, as we are liberated from our own fear, our presence liberates others.
>
> Nelson Mandela[1]

Reference

1   Mandela, Nelson, Inaugural Address, 1994.

8 Awareness and planning

The awareness stage is important in the performance management cycle because we are deciding what will become the basis for measuring success. If this step is given only superficial attention the subsequent stages will all fall short of achieving high performance. How can we build a bridge from 'where we are' if we don't know where the other end is going to arrive?

Performance plans should be challenging and achievable and set as part of a two-way dialogue that seeks to reach agreement and acceptance of the plans by managers and staff.

The planning process

There are four tasks in the planning process:

- defining performance 'outputs' in terms of *outcomes* and *results*.
- agreeing improvements in current performance levels (bridging the 'performance gap').
- agreeing a specific focus.
- agreeing the 'expected range'.

Performance outputs

Any activity or role can be looked at in terms of the outputs of the effort expended, i.e. 'what we produce'. If the activity is chopping logs, the outcome will be a supply of chopped logs and the result will be a warm home. If the person chopping the logs was doing it for someone else then the outcome would be the same, but the result for the log chopper might be in the form of wages. The result for the person paying the log chopper is a warm home. We can see from this simple example that there is always an

Table 8.1   Assessing activity outcomes

Activity	Outcomes
1 Interviewing customer	Customer profiles
2 Analysing customer's needs	Customer's needs lists
3 Assessing marketing approach	Matching products/services to customer needs
4 Customer contacts	Qualifying sales prospects
5 Sales contact	Making a sale
	Not making a sale

outcome and a result from any performance.

Chapter 2 discussed measuring performance in terms of outcomes and results with several examples of how this can be done. This chapter will focus on the steps necessary to decide on the expected outcomes and results for a particular job.

The first step is to look at the job in terms not only of what the performer has to do, but also of the outcomes that will arise from the work. For many jobs this needs to be done once and then amended as the job changes (see Table 8.1).

You can view this analysis as the overall activity of selling with the outcome of making a sale, which from a broad perspective it is. However, by looking at the more detailed activity level it is possible to assess performance at each level and to see more clearly where improvements can be made. But more of this later.

The next step is to examine the results of each outcome (see Table 8.2).

With this level of analysis you can move with confidence to the next step of the planning process.

Table 8.2   Assessing activity results

Outcomes	Results
1 Customer profiles	Clarity about customers
2 Customer's needs list	Focus of attention
3 Matching products/services to customer needs	Informed sales potential
4 Qualifying sales prospect	Focus for time and effort
5 Making a sale	Income for the business
Not making a sale	Loss of time and effort

Agreeing improvements

Without a detailed view of expected performance outputs it is difficult if not impossible to assess and plan for improvements. We are concerned with 'bridging the performance gap' – looking closely at ways in which outputs can be improved. For each of the expected outcomes and results the scope and scale of what is expected has to be planned.

In the example in Table 8.2 it may be that improvements need to be made on the outcome of 'customer's needs lists' and on the result of 'focus of attention'. This might have been identified from reviews which have shown that the 'focus of attention' has been too broad and should be narrowed. It will of course impact on activities which follow and should lead to improved sales, i.e. an improvement in overall performance. Overall improvement is unlikely to occur unless the detailed improvement area is identified and worked on.

Agreeing a specific focus

The third step of the planning process is to agree a specific focus for performance. Having identified areas for improvement it is likely that a specific focus would be how these areas impact on outcomes and results of subsequent activities in the job sequence. To continue our example a specific focus might be to look at how the improvement in the 'customer's needs lists' and the 'focus of attention' leads on to improvements in the 'matching of products/services to customer's needs' and the 'informed sales potential', and so on through the job sequence.

In some organizations the work on sales leads is done by specialist staff who then pass the information on 'qualified leads' to salespeople. In such a situation the careful analysis of activity outcomes and the appropriate focus on areas of improvement is clearer than when all the activities are carried out by the same person. This is one reason why improvements are so hard to achieve in jobs with a complex mix of activities with a variety of outcomes which impact on each other.

Agreeing the 'expected range'

The fourth step in the planning process is to agree the 'expected range' of performance in terms of the outcomes and results included in the plan. A range of performance is recommended rather than a single target. Using a range for a performance indicator shows what is considered satisfactory, so that above the range is high performance, below the range is low performance. It enables both challenging and achievable expectations to be agreed.

Table 8.3   Expected performance ranges

Outcomes	Results	Expected ranges
1 Customer profiles	Clarity about customers	25–35 customers a week
2 Customer's needs list	Focus of attention	1–2 primary needs each 2–4 secondary needs each
3 Matching products/ services to customer needs	Informed sales potential	Match to all primary needs Match to 50% secondary needs
4 Qualifying sales prospect	Focus for time and effort	50%–75% of all matches
5 Making a sale	Income for the business	40%–60% of qualified leads
Not making a sale	Loss of time and effort	60%–40% of qualified leads

In our example we might agree the expected ranges as shown in Table 8.3.

This performance plan enables performers to both focus attention and measure progress in achievement as time unfolds. It is this clarity about what is expected which separates good performance planning from more generalized and less effective 'objective-setting' approaches.

Working to standards

In the example the expected ranges are used as quantitative performance measures and standards for the expected performance. Other standards of a quality nature may also be necessary as well as the quantity standards indicated here. For example we might add quality standards for cancellations and complaints which would provide a balance for the over-energetic sales approaches of some salespeople. These would be added to the performance plan as overall performance measures.

The output focus

So far in the planning process everything has been *output focused*. This is very important because it concentrates attention not on what people do, but what they produce from their doing. It focuses on performance rather than competency. The next phase covers those factors which have an impact on performance and how we include them in the planning process.

The awareness process

Although we have not focused on what people do it is clear that what they do and how they do it impacts directly on performance. It is, therefore, important to examine carefully the five factors of performance (discussed in detail in Chapter 3) and to be aware of what can be done to help performers achieve their plans. There are usually limits to the extent of the improvements that can be made in the five factors and it is useful to look at both improvements and limits (see Table 8.4).

Table 8.4   The five factors of performance

Factors	Improvements	Limitations
The environment The conditions Personal desires Personal state Personal competencies		

The table gives an idea of what data is included in the initial performance plan. It is important that managers and their staff are clear about the impact of these five factors on performance and that performance is planned with awareness of all the possible limitations.

You may see this approach as making allowances for poor performance, but on the contrary where the five factors are taken fully into account performance is usually considerably improved. It is as if the simple acknowledgement of difficulties enables people to address them positively rather than to see them as troublesome obstacles.

Agreeing boundaries

Part of the planning process is to ensure that appropriate boundaries are agreed around the work of each person, not to limit them but to clarify the extent to which they can operate.

Responsibilities

People need to know clearly what aspects of the work they are responsible for, especially when guiding the work of others. List responsibilities under the heading of 'You are responsible for' and then state each element of responsibility. Circulate the information to other people so that everyone is clear who is responsible for what.

Extent of freedom

Too many rules hamper performance, too few rules provide no safeguards against excess. A balance is required between the essential rules for what is prudent and the freedom to be creative. Such a balance is difficult to achieve and most organizations exercise too much prudence and control. There is a good case for relaxation of rules, because it releases individual energy and creativity which are essential ingredients of high performance.

The key is to agree the extent of freedom with each person, in relation to their performance plans. These can be changed as circumstances dictate.

Authority

There will usually be some predefined scope to what people can do. Even when responsibilities and the extent of freedom have been carefully spelt out, it may still be necessary to state the authority levels that they have to work within. Never assume that these are 'understood' – they should be clearly stated.

Barriers

Barriers to performance will probably exist and may have been included in the plans for dealing with the five factors of performance. If barriers exist they need to be recognized and stated and attention paid to how they may be tackled. This is part of the process for 'bridging the performance gap' and should be high in the performer's awareness.

Planning performance support

It is important that performers know what support is available and that managers agree to what they are prepared to give in the way of support. This is particularly relevant in dealing with improvements in 'the environment' and in 'the conditions' in which the performance is to take place. Improvements in these factors will have already been planned and managers should state their part in seeing that they take place.

The extent of support for providing people with challenges and new experiences also needs to be stated, and the way that managers and their staff intend to 'work together' to achieve high performance.

A blueprint for 'bridging the performance gap'

The awareness and planning stage of the performance management cycle should result in a written statement (blueprint) of what is expected and what has to be done to achieve expectations (see Table 8.5).

Using this document as a blueprint provides managers and their staff with a clear indication of expectations and the factors that will impact on achieving them. In this way we can start the performance management cycle with awareness and a clear focus.

The awareness and planning meeting

At first sight these suggestions might appear to be extensive and onerous, but this need not be the case if the work is shared and if managers and staff treat it as a joint effort.

The awareness and planning meeting is a two-way process. Preparation is necessary for both the performer and the manager each of whom has seven key things to do before the meeting.

Performer's preparation

Imagine yourself as the performer. Using Table 8.5 as a guide:

1   Produce your own performance plan in draft.
2   Consider what you need to do to improve your performance.
3   Decide what aspect(s) of your performance to focus on and why.
4   Define overall what you think will be expected of you in the future.
5   Define the boundaries you expect to work within.
6   Indicate the support you expect to receive.
7   Prepare a list of questions and comments you may wish to raise with your manager.

Manager's preparation

Imagine you are the manager. Using Table 8.5 as a guide:

Table 8.5 Performance plan blueprint

Performance plan Page 1

PERFORMANCE OUTPUTS			
Activities	Outcomes	Results	Performance measures

THE FIVE FACTORS
The environment
The conditions
Personal desires
Personal state
Personal competencies

Performance plan Page 2

BOUNDARIES
Responsibilities
Extent of freedom
Authority
Barriers

PERFORMANCE SUPPORT
Factors of performance
Challenges and experiences
Working together

1 Produce a draft of what you expect the performer to achieve.
2 Prepare a list of areas for improvement.
3 Focus on strengths and improvements, not on faults and weaknesses.
4 Define what you expect from the performer in the future.
5 State the performer's boundaries clearly.
6 Indicate how you plan to support them.
7 Prepare a list of questions and comments you may wish to raise with the performer.

The awareness and planning meeting should be:

A MEETING OF EQUALS.

During the meeting managers and their staff should tell each other openly and honestly what they are thinking and feeling about the plans for their future performance. This is the moment to express fears and concerns about expectations. The aim is clarity and agreement and it cannot be achieved in an atmosphere of apprehension and avoidance.

Managers and staff have different responsibilities, but they both share one overriding aim:

TO BRIDGE THE PERFORMANCE GAP.

9   Development and performance

Personal development

The performance management cycle represents a process of searching for and finding improvements in performance, in other words of 'bridging the performance gap'. Part of this process concerns personal development – individual abilities and attributes. Some of this development comes from the performance support and the balance from self-development, on-the-job training and coaching.

Self-development is not an excuse for managers to do nothing and leave it all up to their staff. Performers should take responsibility for getting the opportunities they need to develop, and make a commitment to their own growth with the help and support of their managers.

Guided development, i.e. on-the-job training and coaching, is not an excuse for staff to do nothing and to wait for someone else to develop them. It is a supportive approach which helps them to take the opportunities available to them.

For development to succeed people need:

- to have their personal *aspirations* taken seriously
- to be *challenged* in all aspects of work and life
- to be provided with *opportunities* for development
- to have clear development *objectives*
- to believe in their own *potential*.

Aspirations

An aspiration can be defined as

a strong desire for high achievement.

It is something that all high performers possess. Where it comes from and why some people have it and others don't is a mystery. But if the individual aspirations of people are not taken seriously they will tend to stop having them or tone them down and performance will suffer.

Challenges

Most high performers enjoy and seek out challenging situations and activities. At work junior members of staff could be challenged by being asked to deal with some activity, like talking to local school-leavers about the importance of the organization's work and the particular benefits their organization brings to society. Students will listen more attentively to someone nearer their own age. A branch manager could be challenged by being asked to chair the next regional managers' meeting.

What about challenges in life? These are just as important in motivating people to be high performers. My current challenges are to learn to speak French, and to write a humorous book about my exploits learning to ski.

Opportunities

Of course we all need opportunities to develop. Some we can create for ourselves in our own time, others we need to be allowed the freedom and time to explore. Although we need to make a personal commitment, we also need a commitment from others to support us. At work this will be our manager and our colleagues, at home it might be our partner.

Opportunities may be jointly created, such as training followed by relevant work experience. No matter how the opportunities are created we have to make the best of them. Nobody else can do it for us.

Development objectives

Development opportunities are unlikely to happen if people don't plan them and set targets.

To be successful your development plans have to be realistic and of immediate benefit, i.e. related to what is happening for you now in your life, and achievable. It is no good aspiring to speak several languages and creating opportunities to learn them, until you can master one extra language. Nor is it of great value to learn something that you cannot apply in practice.

Your development plan should include three questions:

- How do I want to improve?
- What is my action plan (assuming anything is possible)?

- What training do I need to prepare myself?

The answers to these questions are the beginnings of your personal development plan. Work on your plan so that you begin to make it happen.

Potential

Why limit yourself? We are all unlimited in our potential. However, there are factors in life that we have to acknowledge as limiting our realization of our potential, 'potential inhibitors':

- lack of self-belief
- lack of belief by others
- lack of opportunity
- lack of support
- lack of commitment.

A good performance management approach should remove, or reduce, these 'potential inhibitors' so that everyone involved can explore their full potential and bring this to bear on their performance. If we can all discover and realize our latent potential there is no limit to our performance possibilities.

Competency development

One of the five factors of performance which impacts on our performance is personal competency, an aspect which is often focused on to the exclusion of many others. It is as if people believe that improving their competency is enough on its own to improve performance. It rarely is and yet it has an important impact on how we perform.

There are two steps towards developing the competencies we need:

- assessing the 'competency gap'
- bridging the 'competency gap'.

Assessing the 'competency gap'

To assess the 'competency gap' it is necessary to know what competencies are needed to perform people's jobs. This is the *job competency profile*. It lists the knowledge and skills needed to perform jobs and may be compiled from a schedule of standard competencies or built up separately for each job. Certain jobs make a greater demand on certain competencies and so it may be desirable to focus attention on key or priority competencies.

The second requirement is a *personal competency profile* which lists the current competencies that people possess. It should be a complete statement of all competencies and should not be aimed at a particular job match.

When the two profiles are ready they can be compared to see the extent of the 'competency gap'. The comparison may indicate that some competencies are missing and/or that others need enhancing. It is also likely that people will possess competencies beyond what they need for their particular jobs. If there is any gap in key or priority competencies then that is where development action should first be focused.

Bridging the 'competency gap'

Developing competency is a mixture of training, coaching, practice and experience. These four are accompanied by an increase in self-esteem and confidence as the new competency becomes increasingly fluent. There is a competency cycle which moves from:

- 'unconscious incompetence' – not being aware that you can't do something – to
- 'conscious incompetence' – being aware that you can't do something – to
- 'conscious competence' – learning to do it and becoming aware that you can do it – and finally to
- 'unconscious competence' – you become adept at it.

The approach to developing competencies should be planned as part of the development and performance stage of the performance management cycle. Make a plan for each competency (see Table 9.1). These plans are the 'worksheets' that help us to implement the blueprint of our performance plan.

Table 9.1   Basic competency development worksheet

Competency	
Training	Practice
Experience	Coaching

It is probably a good idea to concentrate on one competency at a time. This does of course depend on the circumstances of the particular situation.

Performance

Development does not take place in a vacuum. Trainees need the opportunity to practise what they have learned, otherwise it is lost. As they become more practised they need to increase their confidence by exploring ways to use their new skills. This is experience, during which they will need help and guidance, that is, coaching. All of this happens as people perform. So development and performance are very closely linked and need to be seen as an integration of all that has been learned.

Awareness

Being aware of what is happening during performance is an important part of the development process. Reaching a state where skills are so finely honed that people can operate with 'unconscious competence' happens because they have been acutely aware of what they are doing during their development.

To gain this level of awareness calls for considerable concentration and attention to the task in hand. It is here where organismic learning is at full stretch. All our senses are called into play to support our development. Managers who are coaching people must also be highly focused on what is happening. With this high level of awareness it is possible to review performance with a clear mind and to give and receive feedback which aids our development.

All performance is a development opportunity. Sometimes the repetitive nature of what we are doing and our lack of interest, i.e. going through the motions, has little if any developmental value. This is why awareness is so important, because without it we don't focus and we don't develop.

Needs

During performance we will need support and guidance. As we become more experienced and more confident we are able to be self-supporting and eventually reach a stage where we can support others.

It is a fact of life that people don't like asking for help. It seems to be seen as a sign of weakness. One of the expressions I most often meet in my work is, 'I like to manage on my own. I don't want to be a nuisance, asking for help all the time.' This is understandable and yet it is very hard for even the most attentive coach to know exactly when people need help and exactly what help they need.

During the development planning stage people can state clearly what they think they need and this can be added to the competency worksheet as a list of needs. Such a clear statement of intent can overcome any feelings of inadequacy that might be triggered by asking for help.

As learning and confidence increase the list reduces, but it never entirely disappears. Getting people to acknowledge this is very difficult. It has been my experience that the three things people, especially senior managers, find hardest to say are:

'I am wrong',
'I don't know,'
'I need help'.

If we wait until we are out of our depth before we shout 'Help!' we might drown.

Outputs

As performance continues it is essential to monitor outputs so that they can be compared to the original performance plan. If a particular period of performance is concerned primarily with development then output records should clearly indicate this. It is unlikely that we will achieve the planned levels of performance during early development.

It can be helpful to set a date by which we expect full performance levels to be achieved. This can be added to the competency development worksheet together with the list of help we might need. Our competency development worksheet might then look like Table 9.2.

Satisfaction

Satisfaction is hard to describe but very pleasant to experience. When you develop some new skill and use it to achieve what you want to achieve you experience a sense of pleasure and a feeling of awe for your unlimited potential. This is satisfaction. It is fostered by affirmation from others about your achievement. Satisfaction is the ultimate and most valuable reward of personal development.

Table 9.2   Extended competency development worksheet

Competency:	
Training	Practice
Experience	Coaching
Development needs:	
Full performance to be achieved by:	

10   Performance review

A performance review is a discussion between performers and their managers about how well they are performing. It is not an appraisal that seeks to rate or grade performance. It is a means by which progress in 'bridging the performance gap' can be determined.

The importance of performance reviews

Performance reviews are important for four reasons:

- They are instrumental in keeping everyone's focus on the performance plans.
- They provide an opportunity for dealing with difficulties that might be preventing people from performing at their best.
- They provide managers with an opportunity to acknowledge the progress performers are making towards achievement of their performance plans.
- They provide an opportunity for dealing with changing circumstances.

The performance review is an essential stage in the performance management cycle and is designed to maintain both performers' and managers' motivation and commitment.

Performance reviews are for assessing progress, i.e. the 'stage posts' of the performance plans, and discussing any ways to improve performance. The objective is to acknowledge performance and to encourage performers to improve wherever they can. This acknowledgement and encouragement comes not only from managers, but also from performers' own knowledge and opinion of how well they are doing.

During the performance review all aspects of performance should be considered with the emphasis on outputs, in order to clarify to what extent the 'performance gap' is being bridged. It is useful if performers have their own ideas about how they are progressing and the areas where they think they can improve. The key in the review is to see how far the bridge is spanning the gap, not how deep the chasm is.

The focus is on improvement and achievement, not on finding fault or criticism. Of course everyone encounters difficulties from time to time and these need to be discussed openly and honestly. The performance review is not the time and place to deal with matters of discipline. There should be a completely separate procedure for dealing with discipline and this should be used when necessary.

An honest expression of progress, difficulties, and help that might be needed is essential if reviews are to be successful in leading to improved performance.

The timing of performance reviews

Performance reviews should be a regular feature of normal working practices and could be arranged by managers, requested by performers, or dictated by circumstances.

Arranged by managers

When managers think it would be helpful to review the performance of one of their staff, they should:

- suggest the need for a review and why
- give the performer time to think about it and prepare
- agree a time and place for the review.

Remember, a 'quick chat' is not a review. Performers should know whether the review is going to cover all or just one particular aspect of performance.

Requested by performers

Performers should always participate fully in all aspects of managing their own performance. They should be able to ask their managers for a performance review when they think it is necessary. This might be for several reasons:

- they think it is a long time since their last review
- they want to discuss some dificulty

- they think there are changes which are affecting their performance
- they want to check their manager's opinion about how well they are doing.

When performers request a review they should explain why they want it and what they hope to gain from it. Managers should treat requests as seriously as they would expect staff to treat their suggestion for a review.

Dictated by circumstances

Changes can occur which affect the basis and focus of previously prepared performance plans. When this happens performance plans should be reviewed for all the people affected by the change, and should be included in the implementation plan of the change.

Performance reviews which deal particularly with changing circumstances are a special kind of review which may involve changing performance plans. These could be when:

- people are promoted or transferred to a new job
- there is a new line manager
- the objectives of the business unit change
- a new product is launched
- there is a new focus for activities.

Promotion or transfer to a new job will result in a revision of performance plans. A review should be carried out by the performer's old manager to record performance in their old job and they need to have a planning meeting with their new manager to establish what is expected of them in their new job.

A performance review is important when *managers change*. New managers will need to meet their staff and understand what is expected of them in their performance plan. New managers may also want to hear what their staff have to say about their own performance and to explore ways in which they might improve. In fact a series of performance review meetings is a very good way for new managers to get to know staff and to learn about their performance plans. Managers can read through the performance plans but this is a poor substitute for face-to-face meetings with the focus on performance.

From time to time the original *objectives of business units* change to reflect a responsive attitude to the marketplace and it may be necessary to amend the performance plans of some or all of the people in the unit. If this happens they should have the opportunity of participating in the changes through a performance review discussion.

It is important for organizations to remain competitive, by *introducing new products* to meet market needs, or by reacting to new legislation. Performance plans may need to be changed and a performance review is a good way to make and record the changes.

During any given planning period the *focus of activities may change* and people's original performance plans will no longer be appropriate for current business needs. Once again a performance review will enable the original plans to be adapted in response to business needs.

This is not an exhaustive list of circumstances which might indicate the need for a performance review, but it underlines the message that the performance management cycle remains constantly alive to the changing needs of the organization.

Steps in the review process

The review process should provide a clear picture of what is happening and should determine the extent of the 'performance gap', so that improvements can be made and performance plans can be achieved. There are three steps in this process:

- performers' self-assessment
- dealing with difficulties
- providing performance support.

Performers' self-assessment

Self-assessment is when people make their own judgement about their performance in relation to four factors:

- How well am I achieving my outputs?
- How well am I developing?
- What impact are the five factors having?
- How well am I contributing to my team?

This assessment reflects the information on the performance plan and the competency development worksheet, as well as any other relevant points.

Self-assessment is a mixture of measurement and opinion.

First, performers assess how well they are achieving their outputs. If they are not being fully achieved then they should consider how far they are towards achieving them. It is important to be precise in terms of actual performance and comparing it with the performance measures.

Secondly, performers should answer the question: 'What can I do to improve the way I am performing?' They should think about what they are doing and how they might change their approach to make it more effective. They can think of additional things, ignoring for the moment whether they have the time or the opportunity to do them. This includes examining how well their development is going and whether or not the four aspects of training, practice, experience and coaching are being fully carried through.

The third question performers must ask themselves is, 'What is getting in the way of my achieving my performance plans?' It doesn't matter at this point whether or not they can see any way of overcoming these barriers. It helps if these difficulties can be related to the five factors of performance that have previously been discussed.

Performers should also think about the ways in which they contribute to the team. Then prepare notes about how they could improve their contribution.

In all these four areas the performers' self-assessment is an important part of the performance review discussion. Nobody else knows as clearly as the individuals themselves what they are doing in their daily work. Of course managers and colleagues may have different ideas about other people's performance which can be discovered if people talk to their managers and colleagues about their own performance.

Self-assessment is an important part of the whole performance management cycle. It should be carried out at regular intervals and always before a performance review.

It is very useful for everyone to keep their own performance log in which they note down their self-assessment and record each time they do something really well. People can keep a record of difficulties they are encountering and how they are dealing with them. These performance logs will be a valuable source of information for reviews and coaching sessions.

Dealing with difficulties

We all have difficulties in performing well. Sometimes we are aware of them and can deal with them, but often others may be more aware than we are about the difficulties we are having. We either recognize a problem ourselves or someone else, usually our manager, draws our attention to them.

If we don't deal with difficulties as soon as we are first aware of them, they can become an increasing problem. The longer we struggle the more daunting the resolution appears. People with difficulties should tell their managers about them and ask for a performance review. Conversely, a manager who notices a member of staff having difficulties should suggest a performance review. In this way difficulties can be handled in a supportive and non-critical way.

When we are criticized for something with which we are having difficulty it is hard to present the problem to our manager. We all shy away from criticism. We need support in overcoming the difficulty. Non-critical feedback is excellent support because it uses the difficulty as a basis for doing something different.

These difficulties are the things that get in the way of people achieving their performance plans, and can fall into any of the five factors of performance: the environment, the conditions, personal desires, personal state, and personal competencies. What starts as a performance difficulty can, if ignored, become a matter of discipline. When this happens it has to be dealt with outside the performance management system by following the disciplinary procedures. It should be clear to everyone when a difficulty reaches the disciplinary status.

Regular performance reviews which focus on difficulties can often avoid the issue becoming a matter of discipline, but this depends on performers' attitude and commitment to performance and management's attitude to support and encouragement. With the right approach issues of discipline can be avoided and performance improved.

Performance support

To achieve performance plans and to work at their best people need the support of their organization, their manager, and their colleagues. They cannot do it on their own. Unless people work together and support each other nothing of benefit occurs. But support not only comes from outside. We are all capable, to some degree, of supporting ourselves. In fact if we couldn't support ourselves we would die.

Performance support is also both given and received. We cannot work closely with other people without giving them the support they need, or receiving the support they give us. However, many of our support needs go un-met, mostly because we are unable to state clearly what we want. In fact even in the most supportive environment it is still hard to say 'I need help'.

There are four important aspects of support: the support I give, the support I receive, and the sources of this support from myself and from the environment which includes other people. Table 10.1 shows these four aspects of support in the form of a matrix.

Not everyone is open to either giving or receiving support. People tend to

Table 10.1 Performance support matrix

	Support I give	Support I receive
Self-support	I can trust and accept who I am and I have the confidence to be fully myself at all times.	If I am open to receive the support others offer me then I can strengthen my self-support.
Environmental support	I can help to create an environment that supports me and others and allows us to risk being fully ourselves.	When I am in a supportive environment I can relax my guard and concentrate on being fully myself.

operate at one or other end of a spectrum which goes from the extremes of 'not supporting' others to only ever 'being supported' by others.

Within this spectrum there are further extremes. At one end are the 'supporters' who only seem able to give support and find it impossible to ask for, or receive support. At the other end are the 'supported' who only seem able to receive support and never give any. From time to time, for example when we are ill, we may experience these extremes, but most of the time we function somewhere in between.

Many people at work try to appear self-contained and fully self-supporting, leaning towards the 'supporter' end of the scale and not wanting to appear needy. But if we all act like this then the environment becomes non-supporting because nobody is around to receive support, and if no one needs it we cannot give it.

So to be fully supported and fully supporting we have to answer two questions:

● What do I need from others to help me perform?
● What can I give to others to help them perform?

Support is as much about giving as getting and people should give their colleagues the very best they can. This will create a supportive environment. Remember, we can only give what others want and are willing and able to receive.

Exercise – Giving and receiving support

This exercise helps you to examine the pattern of support you experience in your work. By looking at the support you give and receive, and to and from

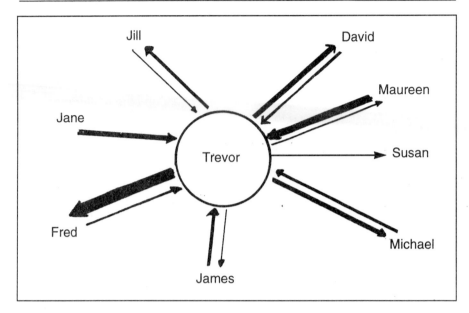

Figure 10.1   Giving and receiving support

whom it flows, you can see how supportive your working environment is.

First draw a circle in the centre of a blank piece of paper. Write your name in the circle. Then write the names of all the people you work with round the edge of the page. Next draw lines with an arrow pointing to the people to whom you give support, and then lines to yourself from the people who give you support. If there is only a little support flowing draw a very thin line, if lots of support draw a very thick line. Your support picture should look like Figure 10.1. Whatever it looks like it will be illuminating for you.

Managers often resist or object to the notion of giving and receiving support. It is as if we all have to stand alone totally self-supporting. It is a good feeling to be self-supporting and it is a good feeling to ask for and get the support we need when we need it.

Windows on support

Managers are often defensive about needing support. Most managers readily accept other people's need for support and see the importance of their role in providing it. This defensiveness seems to stem from the idea that people are supposed to be able to function without support and that only the weak and vulnerable need support. This idea is wrong. No one can function effectively in this world without support.

Support is more a matter of respect and being approved of. It is feeling that I am trusted and that people will be straight with me.

Without support there are three things I cannot say:

I don't know
I am wrong
I need help

Support is to encourage me or lend me strength especially when I am in difficulty.

I need support when I am struggling – not to do things for me, but to help me to do things for myself.

Support is not a crutch, although sometimes I may need a crutch. Support is not a place to hide, although sometimes I may need a place to hide. Support is what you give me that enables me to be honest and true to myself.

When I am told I am wrong, even when I am, I feel put down, belittled. When it is suggested that I could do something in a better or more appropriate way I feel encouraged, supported and motivated.

Good managers know that by supporting their people they, in turn, support their managers.

Leadership does not mean managing, controlling and manipulating people. It means helping and guiding people in the most appropriate direction and helping them to discover their own strengths.

Figure 10.2   Windows on support

The comments in Figure 10.2 demonstrate the variety of ways of looking at support.

Performance reviews and support

Performance reviews are an excellent way of discovering the support people need and that they are not asking for. Most of us struggle to admit that we need help. It is as if we are belittling ourselves when we say 'I can't do this on my own'. Of course the opposite is true, because it takes courage to be open and honest enough to admit we need help.

One of the greatest problems that stands in the way of people receiving the support they need is the 'task orientation' of most jobs. It seems that nothing must get in the way of doing the job. In fact doing nothing about performance reviews is exactly what does get in the way. Without regular reviews people are likely to blunder ahead trying to 'make do' without the help and support they need.

Managers who are 'too busy' to spend time reviewing performance and coaching and supporting their staff are not managing performance. At best they are 'task managers', focused on getting things done, rather than 'people managers' who are focused on helping their staff to perform which includes getting things done.

Exercise – The benefits of performance reviews

In Table 10.2 indicate how important the benefits of a performance review would be for you personally. Rate the importance from 1 – Very important, to 5 – Not important.

Bridge building

The primary use of performance reviews is to help people build bridges towards their performance plans. One of the key aspects of successful bridge building is not to look down. If we focus on the depth of the chasm, the distance we have to go seems much further than it really is.

The key to building performance bridges is to build effective supports that will allow people to progress at the speed and distance appropriate to their desires and capabilities. Pushing people to jump across 'performance gaps' will lead to fear and resistance. When people are pushed they only see the depth of the chasm and the dangers they face.

Bridge building is all about encouragement, support and taking small steps forward. The occasional leap may occur and when it does it should be welcomed as a bonus.

Table 10.2 Benefits of performance reviews

BENEFITS	1 2 3 4 5
They will help my manager and I to plan for activities that will help me to achieve my performance plans.	
They will help me to plan where I can make improvements in my day-to-day work.	
I will be able to see clearly where to direct my efforts.	
I will feel that my performance is being acknowledged.	
They will make it possible for me to discuss difficulties.	
They will be an opportunity for me to discuss the effect changes are having on my work.	
They will enable me to see if my own ideas about my performance are the same as my manager's.	
They will enable my manager to more readily express concerns about areas of my work.	
They will improve the communication I have with my manager.	
They will help me to maintain my motivation and commitment.	

11 Coaching

Nick Faldo is perhaps the best golfer in the world. He manages to maintain his peak performance for long periods of time. This is due to his inherent talent and skills, his commitment to practising and his coach David Leadbetter.

Even with this obvious enormous talent, Faldo's top-class performance is undoubtedly aided by the motivation, inspiration, observation and support provided by his coach.

Many managers and top executives are expected to perform at very high levels of competence continuously and consistently, regardless of the difficult events and problems which arise every day, and to do this without the support of a coach. Top sportspeople would not even contemplate such a situation.

Coaching does not involve giving advice or telling people what to do. On the contrary, it is an approach to personal support which helps people to focus attention on those areas of their performance where there are opportunities for improvement. Through asking awareness-generating questions and by observing and commenting on performance the effective coach is able to provide the kind of feedback that highlights and hones their client's performance. The effective coach can also act as a sounding board to explore alternative options and as someone to listen without having any personal angle to pursue.

Coaching is empowerment

Perhaps the most important aspect of coaching is getting people to believe in themselves. The idea that *what they are trying to achieve is possible* is central to effective coaching. It also encourages individuals to apply their existing knowledge and skills more effectively and thus improve their performance.

There is a distinct difference between training and coaching, although the two are often confused. The following definitions indicate the basis of the difference between them:

Training – The provision of opportunities for people to *gain new knowledge and skills*.

Coaching – The provision of support and guidance for people to *use their existing knowledge and skills more effectively*.

In coaching there is no intention to 'train', but during coaching people may find that their understanding and/or insight improves and that they discover more about the subtleties of applying their knowledge and skills to their work.

The stages of coaching

Coaching is a cycle of activities which focuses on the whole or just a part of the job of the person being coached. The focus is often decided upon as a result of a performance review. In fact the assessment stage in the coaching cycle is a performance review.

The coaching cycle consists of five stages (see Figure 11.1).

Agreeing aims

The first stage of the coaching process is to agree the aims of the coaching

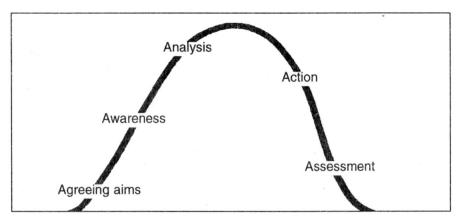

Figure 11.1   The five stages of coaching

activity, which need not be a lengthy process. The focus should be on that part of the individual's performance that has been selected for attention, and the primary aim will be to improve performance. For coaching to be successful, agree upon more detailed specific aims for the various elements which make up the area identified for improvement. These aims should be measurable and have agreed completion dates.

Awareness

Managers who are operating as coaches, and the recipients of the coaching, should be aware of what is happening as the performer performs. One role for coaches is to guide performers to a clearer understanding of what they are doing. Making assumptions does not help to increase awareness, in fact it can deflect attention away from where it is most needed. Coaches should talk with the people being coached about what they see happening and try to get performers to understand and agree.

Clarity about *what* is happening at the moment is perhaps the most important aspect of coaching. It is not necessary to know *why* it is happening, but how we can do things differently to improve. Knowing what is happening now is the starting point in recognizing the 'performance gap' between where we are and where we want to be, and in identifying the missing ingredients.

Analysis

Analysing what has been observed and what the performer has experienced is the next step. From this analysis coaches and performers can discuss and evaluate the options to determine what can be done differently to improve.

If the analysis is an effective two-way interaction between the coach and the performer, there is every chance that performers will recognize what they can do for themselves.

Remember, during the analysis stage it is essential that both coach and performer learn from the experience. It is not about finding fault or focusing on errors.

Action

The 'action' stage of coaching is an opportunity to learn rather than a test of ability. To make the action effective performers should know clearly what is expected of them and have the support and experience of their coach. The encouragement to try new skills is essential for improving performance.

Taking action is the essence of performance.

Assessment

The final stage of the coaching process is the assessment of the performance in a form that will help performers to improve. Positive encouragement, by being honest and giving non-critical feedback, is important.

Whatever system of assessment is agreed and understood it should be used as a review mechanism to evaluate the degree of success achieved, the learning experienced and further opportunities for improvement. The assessment also enables coaches to reflect on their own learning and development.

I recommend doing the assessment in three stages:

- an overall evaluation of the performance
- some indication of its good elements
- suggestions for improvement.

Try to recognize that the people who are being coached may often have greater skill and ability than the coach, but that without the critical eye and the knowing experience of the coach they may find it difficult to improve. For example, Wimbledon finalists are usually far better tennis players than their coaches, but the coaching can make all the difference. The idea of coaching is that someone who has knowledge and experience is trusted to help someone less experienced but with skill and talent to develop.

Asking questions

Successful coaching is achieved by asking questions rather than by giving technical advice, though this may be done as well. Asking questions is part of the bridge-building process that helps people to manage their own performance. The information that performers hold in their minds and bodies about what is going on can be tapped and harnessed for their personal growth. Table 11.1 shows a schedule of questions for the five stages of coaching.

Scenario – the service and sales meeting

Michael is running a service and sales meeting for the first time, having attended a course on running meetings. He is aware that it is part of a coaching exercise. The scenario starts before the meeting and continues afterwards. Margaret is Michael's manager. They are having a discussion about the meeting and the way Margaret will support Michael.

Table 11.1 The coaching process

Process stages	Questions asked leading to	Information gained
Agreeing aims	What are we trying to achieve? When are we going to do it? How will we know we've succeeded?	Clear objectives Agreed dates Measurement
Awareness	What is happening now? What have you done so far? What are the consequences? What do we want to be different?	Clear picture of current actions Effect of current actions Gap between where we are and where we want to be
Analysis	What can we change? What are the options? How can we change it? What are the risks? What are the barriers?	Identify possibilities Broaden vision Seek solutions Evaluate choices Obstacles to overcome
Action	What are we going to do? Who is going to do what? When are we going to do it? What do we need to help us?	Clear action steps Agree responsibilities Agree milestones Determine support
NOW DO IT		
Assessment	What actually happened? Was this what we wanted? What have we learned? How can we improve?	Clarify outcomes Evaluate degrees of success Discoveries made Establish further potential

Margaret	The important thing about the meeting is that it is a basis for you to develop your skills. I will be here to offer support and encouragement and afterwards we can discuss how it went, share our views and agree how to take it further.
Michael	I'm feeling very nervous about the meeting, and about getting stuck, or having problems.
Margaret	That's quite understandable. I was nervous at my first service and sales meeting, but I found that by preparing

thoroughly and using what I had learned at my course I didn't get stuck. I don't think you will either if you do the same. And remember, I'll be available.

Michael	Thanks. It helps to know that.
Margaret	OK, so at this stage we are not focusing on any particular aspect of running meetings. We want to see how you do in all areas. I expect that you will handle some aspects well and others perhaps not so well, but of course we don't know what these are at the moment.
Michael	Thanks. I think I'm ready now.

Two days later the staff are gathered for the weekly service and sales meeting.

Margaret	Good afternoon everyone, whilst I am attending the meeting this week Michael is going to lead it. OK Michael, over to you.
Michael	Thanks Margaret. Well I suggest we start by ... Oh, before we do, can I check that everyone has seen the sales figures?

There is general agreement and then Michael continues.

Michael	Well, perhaps I can ask you, Geoff, to comment about the figures for personal loans.
Geoff	It's quite clear that our customers are not getting the message about our competitive rates at the moment. I think we need to change our advertising.
Michael	That may be so, but does that explain why we are so far behind target?
Geoff	*In a somewhat aggressive tone* – No, not completely. The referrals haven't really established the customers' needs, so we waste a lot of time sorting out what they really want. Anyway, why pick on me? Other areas are way down as well.
Michael	I wasn't picking on you. It just seemed that you were making excuses rather than saying what the difficulties are. You have given two reasons neither of which have anything to do with you. What I would like to hear at the

next meeting is what you can do about it, not what you can't. Now, Peter, how about the mortgage side of things?

Peter	Well, we have had several difficulties. First we have had staff problems because of flu, and second we don't have sufficient information on the new mortgage package, and don't tell me these are excuses because they are the facts.
Michael	OK, OK, calm down. I just want us to focus on what we can do.
Peter	Well, your attitude isn't helping.
Michael	I'm sorry if that's how you feel, but I am keen to make sure we agree some action, rather than listen to a lot of excuses for poor performance.
Peter	It's all right for you to play high and mighty. Credit cards are easy to sell.
Michael	That's not fair …
Margaret	Michael, we don't seem to be progressing in this area. Perhaps we can move on.

The meeting continued until everyone had reported and each individual had agreed action for the following week. Michael then closed the meeting. Afterwards he met Margaret in her office.

Margaret	Well, how do you think it went?
Michael	Not so good. I got really tense and Peter didn't help.
Margaret	OK. On the plus side you got clear action plans sorted out for everybody, and you didn't just accept their excuses. However, there were some obvious difficulties. Now, what I want you to do is to go over the meeting in your mind and think about what you could have done differently, especially in the way you interacted with your colleagues. Let's meet on Wednesday to talk about it.
Michael	Yes, OK. Thanks Margaret.

At their Wednesday meeting Margaret and Michael agreed that there are at least six different areas in which Michael could improve. To address all six issues at this stage would be offputting for Michael and instead of feeling encouraged he may feel discouraged. Michael and his coach Margaret have decided that the first important step for him to take is to improve the way that he handles the interaction between people at the meeting. Margaret agrees that Michael needs to start here because it will affect everything else he tries to improve.

At his second service and sales meeting Margaret and Michael have agreed that of the six areas for attention he should focus on his interactions with other people. The six areas are:

- opening the meeting and defining aims
- focusing on key issues and keeping to the point
- dealing with confrontation
- making interventions
- *interactions with others*
- summarizing the meeting.

Michael	Hello everyone. Margaret has asked me to lead the meeting again. What do you think we should focus on today?
Betty	I would like us to consider more sales training.
Michael	OK. Anything else?
Peter	Yes. I'd like a policy decision on the use of the tax notes that were circulated this week. Are we going to give them to customers or not?
Michael	I don't think we can make a decision like that here ...
Peter	Well somebody needs to.
Michael	*Glaring at Peter* – Any more points to consider?

There are no further suggestions and so Michael continues.

Michael	Perhaps we could go round the table and ask each of you to report on sales for the week.
Betty	OK, I'll start.

Each person reports to the meeting. Michael listens, takes notes and asks one or two questions to clarify points. When everyone has spoken he asks for general comments about sales performance.

Geoff	I don't think we've done too badly considering the current climate.

Michael	What do you mean, Geoff?
Geoff	Well, people are not too excited about investing or borrowing. The whole economy is sluggish.
Michael	That may be, but what are we going to do about increasing sales to our customers? I'm sure there must be scope.
Peter	If we could get our act together, we might stand some chance.
Michael	*With a sharp edge to his voice* – And exactly what is that supposed to mean?
Peter	I think we need more explanatory leaflets and …
Michael	So you don't have to talk to customers? Just send them away with something to read?
Peter	You know I don't mean that.
Michael	Well, what do you mean?
Peter	These tax notes, for example. It's easier to explain when you have something to refer to.
Michael	All right, so what do you suggest for the tax notes?
Peter	I think we should refer to them, and if customers ask for a copy we should give them one.
Mary	Yes, I agree. That's a good point.
Betty	I agree too. It makes sense to do that.
Michael	OK, let's address that issue.

The meeting continues until suggestions for action have been agreed and Michael closes the meeting. He then meets Margaret.

Margaret	Well, how do you think it went this time?
Michael	Better I think, but Peter is still driving me mad.
Margaret	Yes, you did seem to have some difficulty with him, but on the whole I thought your interaction was better this week, and you involved everyone more than at your first meeting.
Michael	But what can I do about Peter?

Margaret	What would you like to do?
Michael	I'd like things to be better between us.
Margaret	Yes, you're right. If we ignore the problem it will only get worse. So how do you think you can improve your contact with Peter?

Margaret then helped Michael to explore the nature of the difficulty and options for making changes.

In each of the scenarios two different things are happening at the same time – the service and sales meeting and coaching. Margaret, the coach, concentrates on the coaching process and the person being coached. Michael should be focusing on the content of the service and sales meeting and learning about his interactions with others.

A step-by-step approach

In coaching it is important not to build too big a span in the learning bridge at each stage of improvement. It is far better to make regular small improvements than to try for one big leap forward. Occasionally big leaps do occur, usually because the coaching process reveals some major insight for the individual.

Because coaching moves in small steps it does not mean that it is a slow process. On the contrary, by focusing on each area in turn rapid improvement can occur. If the whole situation were to be tackled in one go then it would be a slow almost overwhelming battle to improve.

Encouragement and commitment – a partnership

Encouragement and commitment go hand in hand.

- Encouragement which comes from outside. It is an external stimulant to our efforts.
- Commitment comes from within. It is our determination to succeed, to do the very best we can. Without our commitment no amount of coaching will help us to improve.

Together, encouragement and commitment can achieve great things. Without encouragement it is difficult to maintain our commitment, especially when things are not progressing as we would like them to.

People need the encouragement of their coach (manager) on every step of the journey, and sometimes it can be hard for coaches to find encouraging things to say. However, the very least will be for them to encourage their staff for the way they keep trying to improve.

People can also encourage themselves, by telling themselves how well they are doing and taking pride in any and every improvement that they make. This level of self-support is not always easy to summon, but becomes easier as they receive more encouragement from their coaches.

Commitment is an inner drive. Without commitment on both sides there is little point people entering into a coaching agreement. In their endeavours to improve they will face many difficulties which will seem insurmountable without commitment. When we are committed we see things differently. We see difficulties as hurdles to jump, not as barriers to success. When such commitment is in evidence it is not a problem for coaches to be encouraging, but it is very hard to encourage someone who shows no enthusiasm.

Encouragement and commitment are a partnership, just as managers and their staff are a partnership in striving for improved performance.

The key elements of coaching

The four key elements of coaching are encouragement, modelling, step-by-step development and support.

Encouragement

People who are trying to improve their performance need constant encouragement to keep trying. There is no advantage telling someone what they are doing wrong. The important information is what they should do differently to improve.

Modelling

Coaches should be able to model what they want the person they are coaching to do. Watching something and then copying it is one of our primary learning mechanisms. It has to be done with understanding of what is happening so that learners do not misinterpret what they see.

Step-by-step development

Many activities and tasks are quite complex when they are first encountered. Even with experience there are sometimes many things to consider when trying to improve. The good coach will concentrate on one aspect at a time, even if it is obvious that several aspects could be improved. This selection of one element to concentrate on at any one time is an important feature of good coaching.

Support

We all need support and this is never more true than when we are being asked to try things out as part of the coaching process. We have to know that it is OK if sometimes we don't perform well. We have to be supported when we are learning from our mistakes. (See Chapter 10 for more on support.)

With care, attention to detail, and a gentle questioning approach good coaches can help people to reach performance levels that they never thought possible.

12 Performance appraisal

Focusing on performance

Performance appraisal is the area of performance management where the focus on performance is the hardest to maintain. More often than not the appraisal turns into an assessment of the individual rather than their performance. It is often exacerbated by the one-way nature of the appraisal, where managers tell performers what they think of their performance and/or of them. The competency-based approach to performance further clouds the issue by looking at how people perform rather than the outputs they produce.

The purpose of performance appraisal

Performance appraisal is an opportunity for managers to evaluate the performance of their staff. Successful appraisal meetings are a two-way dialogue. Managers have the role of helping performers to understand fully and to accept the assessment of their performance during the appraisal period. It is essential for performers to take full ownership for their performance.

It is never easy to evaluate performance. No matter how objective the appraisal process, there will always be an element of subjectivity. This subjectivity, which is sometimes the result of performers and managers having different perspectives, can be minimized by:

● focusing on performance outputs in relation to required standards and measures previously specified either in the planning phase or the review process

- continuous review, monitoring and recording of examples of performance during the appraisal period
- appraisals being done by the person best positioned to be objective about the performer's performance
- a second appraiser reviewing the appraisal process for fairness and consistency.

The evaluation should be based on performance plans ('blueprints') and development 'worksheets'. The opinion of the performer is a vital factor in evaluating performance. Though it is the appraiser's role to arrive at a final overall evaluation of performance, it is the performer's role to prepare a self-assessment and be ready to contribute fully to the dialogue.

Managers need to listen carefully to performers and show them that they have heard and respect their opinions. The whole appraisal process and its outcomes are largely dependent on managers adopting an open, honest and consultative approach from start to finish.

Scenario – purpose and role of appraisal

Jane and Malcolm are talking about their forthcoming appraisals. They are colleagues who both work for David, their appraiser.

Jane	I am worried about my appraisal next week. What do you think is going to happen?
Malcolm	I expect we will discuss my performance and highlight the good and the bad.
Jane	Oh, I hope there's not much bad in my appraisal.
Malcolm	Well, you should know.
Jane	What do you mean?
Malcolm	Haven't you done a self-assessment yet?
Jane	No, not yet. Do you think it's worthwhile?
Malcolm	I do, and I think it also helps to be aware of what I can expect and how to deal with it.
Jane	Such as?
Malcolm	Well, if I feel I haven't been doing very well in an area of performance I think about it and decide what I could do to improve, which is what David will ask me.
Jane	I see. So you think we can counter any criticism by being ready for it?

Malcolm	No, it's not a case of countering criticism, but of being prepared and being honest enough to face the difficulties you have been having and make improvements.
Jane	But I always feel defensive.
Malcolm	That could be because you are not prepared for the meeting, or because you know there is good reason to be defensive.
Jane	Hey, that's not fair. I work just as hard as everyone else.
Malcolm	Well then, what's bothering you?
Jane	I don't know. I think it's something to do with the idea that someone might think I'm not good enough.
Malcolm	All the more reason for you to prepare for the meeting by thinking about your performance. And provide examples of what you have done well, and what you think you can do better. This is what I think it's about. I don't think David sets out to be critical of you.
Jane	That sounds great, as long as it works like that.
Malcolm	I think it's up to us to make sure it does. I'm just as much a part of this as David is, after all it is *my* appraisal.
Jane	I haven't thought of it like that.
Malcolm	Well, that's how I see it. I intend to make sure I get a fair hearing, and to do that I've got to be fair and honest about my performance.
Jane	So really it's up to me to prepare and say what I think?
Malcolm	Absolutely. That's exactly how it should be.

The performance appraisal meeting is an opportunity for performers to discuss their performance fully and frankly with their appraisers, usually their managers. There are two main aims of the meeting. The first is to arrive at an overall evaluation for the period just ending which reflects a fair and balanced view of the performance. The second aim is to identify those areas where performers can improve their performance in the future.

Appraisal meetings are, or should be, a two-way dialogue. It is the performers' responsibility to fully understand, accept and take ownership for their performance. Performers are the only people responsible for their performance. No one else determines how well they perform.

Preparing a self-assessment

People are generally highly influenced by the opinions of those they work for. They must therefore prepare their own assessment of their performance before looking at their appraiser's opinion. A self-assessment is an important part of preparing for the appraisal. There are six stepping stones to success in self-assessment:

- focus on performance
- gather information on performance
- draft a provisional evaluation (self-assessment)
- think about the meeting and what to focus on
- communicate with appraisers
- prepare mentally.

Focus on performance

There is a natural tendency to allow our personal likes and dislikes to influence our opinions and expectations of people. We cannot always work with people we like, nor can we inhibit our inherent prejudices. What we can do is to focus on performance. Of course people's personal qualities and capabilities will be examined in the evaluation process, but only in relation to how it affects their performance.

Gather information on performance

The formal appraisal meeting probably only happens once a year. This is a long period of time to cover and relying on memory to recall events will not provide an adequate basis for a good appraisal. The first place to look for information will be the performance reviews held during the period, which should indicate areas of good performance and areas for improvement.

It is useful to keep a personal performance diary/log, which need only be a single page, showing both good performance and areas where improvements are possible. All that needs to be recorded is what happens and when.

However it is done, it is important that people enter their appraisal meeting as informed performers.

Draft a provisional evaluation (self-assessment)

Drafting a provisional evaluation will help people to focus on the information they have gathered and the opinions they hold regarding their performance. Use the same form normally used for the evaluation process.

Think about the meeting and what to focus on

The way people react at the appraisal meeting is partly connected with their appraiser's style and partly with what they want to focus on. The appraisal covers much ground which will already be known and agreed by performers and their appraisers. It is both tedious and ineffective to spend time going over all these 'agreed' areas in detail.

It is much better to focus on two specific aspects of performance:

- areas where people have been successful
- areas where people think they can improve.

In focusing on these two areas remember that appraisers may have a different opinion from performers. This does not necessarily mean that performers are being criticized, and it is important that they listen carefully to their appraiser's opinion. Being open to comments and suggestions about their performance is an important step to making improvements. Performers should remain positive and receptive at all times, which helps them to reinforce the points they are making.

Communicate with appraisers

Before the appraisal appraisers should:

- give at least two weeks' notice of the time and place of the meeting
- provide an indication of the areas of performance that they want to focus on.

Performers should also check with their appraisers points about their performance that they think are important, and confirm the form of preparation that is required.

Prepare mentally

The appraisal meeting should be a time and place for performers to enter into a friendly purposeful dialogue with their appraisers about their current performance and future potential.

The atmosphere of the meeting should be friendly, fair, objective, purposeful, encouraging, supportive and smoke free. Performers can help this to happen if they remember that the meeting is *their* appraisal for *their* benefit. It is not an arena for bravado and confrontation. If they approach the meeting in an assured, confident way after careful preparation they will be listened to and their views respected.

The performance appraisal meeting

The time, place and atmosphere of the appraisal meeting are important factors in creating an appropriate environment, which should be:

- private, comfortable and relaxed
- quiet, non-threatening and uninterrupted
- convenient, unhurried and confidential
- informal, friendly and without physical barriers.

There is an art in appraising the performance of others. People develop the skill by a mixture of training and experience. Experienced appraisers will be familiar with the importance of the style and impact of the language they use, and will pay attention to the following:

- taking ownership for what they say – by using 'I'
- being friendly and conversational – by using everyday language
- being positive – by saying what they want rather than what they don't want
- being specific – by using particular examples rather than generalizations
- being active – by discussing action rather than reasons and excuses
- being encouraging – by looking forward to improvements with belief and confidence
- including performers – by focusing on what can be done together to improve

Using this table of ideas will help performers and appraisers to focus on improvements and to avoid being judgemental. It is possible to be non-critical by focusing on performance rather than on people themselves.

The elements of successful appraising

A consultative approach

There is a simple model, or framework, that people can follow to make their appraisal meetings a success, and surprisingly to make them more time effective. This model is called a consultative approach and consists of four elements:

- asking open questions
- listening attentively
- reflecting back what is heard
- responding appropriately.

The model encourages performers to share their thoughts and feelings with other people. By using this consultative approach appraisers can manage the meeting without controlling it and be powerful without disempowering performers.

Inviting the performer's comments

The appraiser's views about an individual's performance are important and can be offered more effectively and more acceptably in the context of what individuals think about themselves. It is better to hear the views of performers before appraisers share their own views with them. This is where the consultative model is very important.

All performance stems from, and is motivated by, the performer's inner drive and self-belief. When we use our knowledge of what people think about themselves as a basis for our comments we achieve three advantages:

- we create a climate of acceptance
- we reinforce the performer's confidence
- we can introduce difficulties in a supportive framework.

The ideal way to start the appraisal meeting is by asking performers to talk about their own assessment of their performance.

Highlighting good performance

Appraisers will find it useful to start on a good note. It is easier, it helps people to relax and it is non-threatening. One way is to ask performers to identify highpoints of their performance during the appraisal period. Wherever possible appraisers should acknowledge performers' good performance. Experienced appraisers know that it is counter productive to use good comments to link directly into criticism.

Pinpointing difficulties and focusing on improvements

Appraisers can raise the issue of poor performance by asking performers where they think they are having difficulties. These areas can then be explored to decide what action the performers can take to improve. Most of the time performers will raise the same difficulties that appraisers have in mind. If they don't, then appraisers can introduce their thoughts in a way which is non-threatening, by using questions to draw attention to other areas, and focus on improvements. Here are four questions that appraisers can use:

- Where do you think you can improve?
- How do you think you can improve?
- When do you think you can improve?
- What do you need to help you improve?

These questions all bring performers into the improvement process as owners of the improvement, with responsibility for their own actions. Notice that the focus is still on performance and not on the individual, i.e. on what the individual does and not on the person.

Dealing with difficult moments

There are always difficult moments in appraisal meetings. Such moments are nearly always difficult for both appraisers and performers. Sometimes managers are given advice on how to deal with such difficulties by learning about handling 'problem people'. I don't believe such people exist. I believe that there are 'problems' and 'people' and that we can deal with the problems by separating them from the people. Once we have defined and dealt with the problems then we can deal with the people. Table 12.1 shows a few of the more common difficulties appraisers encounter, with suggestions for dealing with them.

Completing the form

It is usual for a form to be completed as a record of the appraisal. Remember, the form is a means to an end, not an end in itself:

- It is a by-product of the meeting.
- It is a useful tool, but the meeting should not be structured around the form.
- It is a record of decisions and actions.

Moving on

Make notes about the areas for improvement that are to be carried forward to the performance planning phase and the completion of the development

Table 12.1   Difficulties in appraisal meetings

Difficulty	Action
Anger	Encourage and listen to the expression of the anger. Anger is always followed by calm. Stay calm and speak quietly.
Disagreement	Listen to the source of the disagreement. Avoid arguing. Isolate the facts from the feelings. Deal with the facts first, then deal with the feelings.
Unresponsiveness	Ask what is not being said. Check that you are asking open questions. Offer a range of possible answers.
Over-talkative performer	Use a pause to intervene to express your interest in what is being said and seek a summary.
Over-talkative appraiser	Shut up.
Very poor performer	Focus on what is happening, not on the person. Get the performer to agree the facts. Agree action for improvement.
Very good performer	Praise their achievement and look for areas of development.
Performer is emotional and/or cries	Ask them to express what they are feeling. Be silent and give them time to relax.

plan where appropriate. Summarise the appraisal meeting by asking performers to prepare an action plan. This creates a sense of continuity and a clear commitment to act on the outcomes of the appraisal meeting.

Scenario – the appraisal

David   Hello Monica.

Monica   Hello David. Where shall I sit?

David   Why don't you sit by the window, and make yourself comfortable?

Monica sits down and waits as David comes from behind his desk to join her.

David   Why don't you start? I'd like to hear what you think about your performance this year.

Monica	Well, generally speaking I'm very pleased.
David	Tell me what you are particularly pleased about.
Monica	Perhaps the most important thing is that I have achieved all the objectives we set, especially the sales of personal loans.

Monica refers to her self-assessment and quotes the figures to David. She is obviously very pleased.

David	Yes, I agree with you. Your results have been excellent. I need to comment about that on your appraisal form. What else?
Monica	Maybe the improvements I've made in my supervision skills. I think I'm getting on with the staff a lot better now than I was six months ago.
David	Yes, I think that's quite noticeable, and I also like the way you have helped Jenny and Mary on the counter.
Monica	Oh, thanks. I just did what seemed necessary.
David	No, it was more than that. I think you went out of your way to help them and they've become more confident with customers because of your efforts.
Monica	In some ways I think they deal with customers better than I do.
David	In what way?
Monica	Sometimes I lose my confidence and I get flustered.
David	Well, tell me what you think is happening.
Monica	I don't like being in a muddle and ...
David	... Tell me what you do like about working with customers.
Monica	I like knowing my stuff and feeling confident to talk to them.
David	And this happens with personal loans?
Monica	Yes, it does.
David	And mortgages?

Monica	No. I am unsure about the different rates and the different types and I get confused.
David	Then what happens?
Monica	I want to finish the interview and I get flustered, so I give them the leaflets to read and suggest they come back again.
David	What would you like to do to change this?
Monica	I would like to be as confident as I am with personal loans.
David	How could you do that?
Monica	Well, I could learn more about mortgages and become more confident, or I could ask Brian to help me because he really knows about mortgages.
David	So there is room for improvement here then?
Monica	Yes there is, and I think I could do it.
David	Yes, so do I. I'll make a note on the form and we'll make some plans later. Perhaps we can turn to your development plan now. Where do you think you have improved most?
Monica	I think I did really well learning about running the sales and service meetings, and now I enjoy them and I seem to get the right response from everyone.
David	Yes, I agree with you. You do it very well now. Are there any other areas you want to mention?
Monica	Well, I seem to do OK generally.
David	Can you be more specific?
Monica	No, not really. I was thinking mainly about the sales and service meetings.
David	And what about the way you react to changes?
Monica	I don't like change, and I know I resist it.
David	So what do you do when changes occur?
Monica	Well, I say what I think ...
David	... and then you get on and make the changes work, even

if you don't like them, which is why I think you handle changes well.

Monica	OK, thanks.
David	What about teamwork? How well do you contribute to the team?
Monica	I think I play my part OK.
David	Could you give me an example?
Monica	Well, the way I help Jenny and Mary.
David	Yes, that's a good example. Are there ways in which you could improve?
Monica	Of course. People can always improve.
David	That's true. How could you improve?
Monica	Hmm ... Perhaps I could be more willing to work late, but I do find this difficult.
David	Anything else?
Monica	I don't think so.
David	What about your contribution at the staff meetings, and your willingness to cover for counter staff?
Monica	Yes, I could probably do better in both these areas.
David	How could you do better?
Monica	Well, in the staff meetings I could be more open and say what I'm thinking, but I don't want to look silly. And I could be more prepared to cover on the counter, but that seems like I'm going backwards.
David	What do you mean – going backwards?
Monica	It took me a long time to get promotion and I don't want to go back on the counter.

Monica sounds angry and disappointed and there are tears in her eyes.

David	What are you feeling right now?
Monica	I'm annoyed that you should bring this up when I feel I've done well this year.

David	Do you think I'm being unfair?
Monica	Yes, I do.
David	So what would you like me to say? You didn't think I was unfair when I told you how well I thought you were doing.
Monica	That's different.
David	Yes it is. I want to see if you will agree to improve your performance by covering on the counter when we are busy.
Monica	That sounds different. It sounds very reasonable.
David	And I certainly don't want you to go backwards.
Monica	OK, I understand.
David	So let's note these two areas as places where you can improve and we'll cover them in the plans for next year. What do you think, is that fair?
Monica	Yes, I think it's fair and I recognize that there are several areas for improvement that I have to work on.
David	OK. So I'll write my overall comment on the form and you can write yours, then we'll have a break and look at planning for next year and check your development plan.

Five keys to appraising success

There are five key aspects to successful appraising: motivation, clarity, improvement, final comments and a beginning.

Motivation

Performers should leave the appraisal meeting feeling encouraged and motivated to improve. This is likely to happen if:

- they feel they have been listened to
- their manager's focus is encouraging and positive
- they have acknowledged and taken ownership for their current performance
- they recognize their potential for improvement
- they feel that their managers are committed to helping them to improve.

Clarity

A good way to end an appraisal is to summarize the areas of good performance and the areas for improvement by focusing on:

- current success
- future potential for improvement.

By doing this it is possible to clarify the outcomes and to gain agreement and commitment. The summary can be in the form of an 'action plan' for the future, which can be incorporated into the performance planning phase, and may need to be addressed in the development plan.

Improvement

Performers should leave the appraisal meeting understanding and accepting the need to continue to improve their performance. The appraisal meeting will have led directly to the current evaluation of performance. But it is wrong to assume that performers will be clear as to what they have to do to improve their performance. Discussing this with them will help to open up the possibilities for them to achieve more.

Final comments

Always check that performers are clear about the outcomes of the meeting by asking them to summarize the key points.

A beginning

There is a strong possibility that performers could see the appraisal as the end of a process because it comes at the end of the period and the content is mostly about what has happened, i.e. looking back. This perspective can be changed by suggesting that, rather than the ending of the current period, it is the beginning of the next.

The appraisal meeting should link directly with the performance planning phase which might, where practical, be the second part of the meeting, after a suitable division.

Overall performance ratings

In reviewing and designing performance management systems I have found a constant demand for some type of overall rating system. The argument seems to revolve around whether there should be four, five or six grades and what to call them, rather than should there be grades at all.

There is no evidence that performance grading serves any purpose other than to provide an easy way of creating some form of performance distribution curve and then linking this to some mathematical formula for pay increases and/or bonuses.

Performance grading is often divisive in terms of motivating and encouraging people to higher performance. The systems for arriving at the grades are also often divisive, in that they are based largely on the subjective opinions of the performer's manager.

The rating process is intended to be fair to everyone and to genuinely reflect performance against plans and expectations at all levels. For this to work the grading system should be as objective as possible and applied equally to all members of staff.

The best system I have encountered works on five levels which are arrived at jointly by performers and managers, based on the achievement of expectations in terms of performance outputs and completion of development plans. The five levels are:

1 Performance consistently exceeds all requirements associated with the job. Quality and quantity of work is of an exceptional level.
2 Performance consistently meets all requirements of the job and regularly exceeds expectation established for the particular role.
3 Performance consistently meets all requirements associated with the job.
4 Performance meets most but not all of the job requirements. Further improvement is required to perform at a successful level.
5 Performance does not meet the standards associated with the job. Performance should be reviewed.

When arriving at an overall performance rating for staff it is vital for managers to follow the five basic principles of:

- fairness – people should receive a rating which reflects their performance in the way they have achieved their plans and met the expectations placed on them, and not in comparison to other people.
- consistency – the application of rating should be the same across all the different business units, departments and companies within the organization.
- flexibility – managers should be able to make assessments in relation to plans and expectations so as to recognize the extent of the individual's personal achievements.
- equality – ratings must be applied with the same care and diligence to all levels of management and staff.

- honesty – ratings must reflect the honest and open appraisal of the individual after listening to and respecting the individual's views.

My own approach is not to use any form of performance rating. It is sufficient to assess performers on an individual basis in terms of how well they have achieved performance plans and what future improvements need to be made. The link between performance and reward does not need a rating system. There are a variety of alternative and more creative ways of doing this (see Chapter 15).

Reflection and learning

Because the appraisal stage of the cycle links directly with the awareness and planning stage of the next cycle it seems that we have rushed through the reflection and learning stage. This does frequently happen. I think there should be a period of time for reflection after the appraisal and before the next awareness and planning stage.

Performers should:

- reflect on their appraisal and what they have learned about their performance
- enjoy the acknowledgement and recognition that they receive for their achievements
- think about how they want things to be different in the future
- focus on how they can improve their performance.

After a period of time they can then move confidently to the next stage of the cycle, having gained some sense of satisfaction from the completion of the previous cycle.

Upward and 360 degree feedback

Several ways have been introduced over recent years which expand the style of appraisal into a less one-way affair. They have been given various names, but the best known are 'upward feedback' and '360 degree appraisal'. Unfortunately both still carry with them the danger of focusing on individuals rather than their performance.

Upward feedback

As the name suggests this approach to appraisal involves staff reporting on their manager's performance. The difficulty with this approach is the clarity with which the expectations are defined. Upward feedback only works if staff focus on how well their managers have supported and coached them during the period. In other words, staff comment on how they have experienced their managers as managers. To move away from this into more general personal comments degrades the value of the feedback.

Chapter 6 of this book looks at an appropriate approach for managers to take to support their staff. If upward feedback were to focus on how well managers had followed this approach then it would benefit both staff and their managers.

360 degree feedback

The 360 degree approach involves performers being assessed by their managers, their staff and their colleagues – feedback coming from all directions, hence 360 degree. Again it is important to define clearly the basis on which each group is giving feedback rather than to make general comments about the person. It is much easier if performers agree with their staff and colleagues about what is expected of them. To operate 360 degree feedback effectively managers should nominate people whose opinions they will listen to and respect, otherwise it will have no impact. Of course, if managers only nominate those people who they know will give them the feedback they want to hear, then the process is pointless.

Anonymous feedback is divisive and gives a distorted view of how people experience their managers. It provides an opportunity for people to be 'open in secret', which is both contradictory and ineffective.

For feedback to be effective, allow the recipients to acknowledge and own what they receive. They need some form of dialogue with the providers of the feedback. Anonymous feedback can be more easily ignored and/or allows people to vent their personal feelings at someone else's expense.

Both 'upward feedback' and '360 degree feedback' can be very effective if time and trouble is taken to define the expectations against which performance is to be assessed. If this is not done, then at best people get an enhanced view of what others think about them, and at worst it becomes nothing more than a slanging match.

The benefits of successful performance management

A well designed performance management system that focuses on bridging the performance gap and on motivating and encouraging people can provide significant benefits, especially if assessment and appraising of performance is done with flair and creativity, emphasising success and improvement rather than failure and correction. The benefits are as follows:

- Performers will
  - know how they are doing
  - know what is expected of them
  - receive recognition and praise
  - be heard and respected
  - receive help and encouragement
  - take ownership for their performance.
- Managers will
  - improve their communications and relations with staff
  - fully understand the performer's contribution
  - get to know the performer better
  - have a consistent approach for giving praise and encouragement
  - be able to deal with problems more effectively
  - learn about the way people perform.
- The organization will
  - have improved performance from its people
  - have a fair and consistent approach to performance management
  - have greater internal flexibility
  - obtain feedback and new ideas
  - link individual objectives to corporate strategy
  - harness the diversity and creativity of its people
  - bridge the performance gap.

Part 3

Performance reward

13 The reward argument

All performance brings reward in some form or another, from a deep feeling of self-satisfaction to the rapturous applause of an appreciative audience. Our performance is often rewarded with payment, and often it is not. The attentive mother nurturing her child does not receive, nor seek, financial reward. The father playing with his young children is more than adequately rewarded with their loving smiles and gurgles of pleasure. The many volunteers working with charities and helping in community projects find reward in being valued and in their own sense of worth.

Reward is found in a wide variety of forms, differing from person to person. Creating, designing and implementing performance reward systems calls for imagination, awareness of individual needs and attention to detail.

The elements of performance reward

There has been much work done on examining what people want or need in the form of reward. Perhaps the best known work is that of Maslow (1954)[1] who produced his hierarchy of needs (see Figure 13.1).

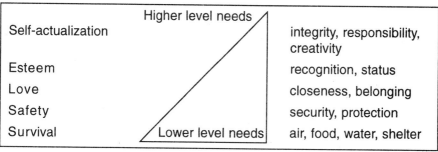

Figure 13.1   Maslow's hierarchy of needs

Herzberg et al.[2] introduced the idea of 'motivation hygiene theory' which indicated that people work first and foremost in their own self-enlightened interest. He divided people's needs into two categories:

Hygiene factors	*Motivators*
Organization culture	Achievement
Management	Recognition
Interpersonal relations	Productive work
Conditions	Responsibility
Pay	Advancement

Herzberg maintained that lack of suitable hygiene factors could demotivate, but their existence had a limited motivational impact.

This early work has since been supported by other pieces of research, notable among which is the subject of the best-seller *In Search of Excellence*, in which Peters and Waterman[3] describe the attributes of high-performing companies. They come out very strongly in favour of treating people decently, fairness, involvement, expecting ordinary people to perform extraordinarily, etc.

With this work as the background it is possible to see how people today have come to expect far more than a 'fair day's pay for a fair day's work'. They expect to be treated well, to be listened to, to be consulted, to be trusted with responsibility, and to be allowed to be creative. In other words they expect the human TOUCH, where touch stands for:

Trust
Openness
Understanding
Consideration
Honesty.

In this environment performance reward can be divided into five main elements:

- satisfaction
- recognition
- appreciation
- status and position
- pay.

Satisfaction

Perhaps the highest level of performance reward is satisfaction with a job well done. Much of this must come from people themselves who know what they are capable of and know when they have delivered their best shot. The environment and conditions can support the chance for satisfaction, but as with Herzberg's hygiene factors they can't create satisfaction.

It is the other performance factors of personal desire, personal state and personal competence which lead to satisfaction. When everything comes together, when people are not deflected from performing at their best, then they can achieve satisfaction. When such satisfying performance is recognized and appreciated, it becomes truly rewarding.

Recognition

Being recognized as a high performer is reward in itself. Knowing that others know that you are a high performer may elicit some embarrassment from you and some envy from them, but it brings with it a sense of self-worth that increases your confidence and probably your competence.

Recognition has to be handled carefully and fit in with the culture of the organization. It is an underutilized element of performance reward and is dealt with in more detail in Chapter 16.

Appreciation

Appreciation is not as public as recognition and yet it is as powerful, if not a more powerful, element of performance reward. Appreciation can be given frequently for the smallest and simplest aspects of performance. From a simple, 'thank you' to a more formal memo or letter, appreciation indicates that performance is being noticed and appreciated. Giving appreciation is one of the most important parts of a manager's job and yet one that is done so ineffectively.

The plea of Blanchard and Johnson[4], in their best-seller *The One Minute Manager*, to spend a minute 'catching people doing something right', seems to have fallen on deaf ears.

Status and position

Status and position satisfy Maslow's esteem or ego needs and is one of the 'higher' level needs that most of us have. Obvious examples of meeting these needs is through the use of high sounding titles and status symbols such as large and/or flashy cars.

Promotion and advancement are seen as an indication of high performance and competence. So there is also a form of recognition in meeting status needs. One of the main problems with this form of reward is delightfully set out in Professor Peter's book, *The Peter Principle*[5] when he puts forward the idea that eventually 'everyone rises to their level of incompetence', at which point they stop rising.

Pay (financial reward)

The issue of pay, all forms of financial reward, is treated in a wide variety of ways. Some put it at the 'lower' level of need and downplay its importance as a form of reward. Others make it the primary focus of reward systems.

There is no doubt that pay is a very important and central part of performance reward. Over the years many different ways have been tried to construct pay systems that motivate people and provide a form of reward that meets the needs of the 'workforce'. Increasingly attempts have been, and are being, made to design pay systems which can be seen to be linked with performance. This important topic is dealt with more fully in Chapters 14 and 15.

Individuality

Of course not everyone reacts in the same way to the different elements of reward. Here are three examples of how people might rank the five elements in terms of importance to themselves.

Dave, a financial adviser:
1 Pay
2 Status and position
3 Recognition
4 Satisfaction
5 Appreciation

Henrietta, a marketing manager
1 Recognition
2 Status and position
3 Appreciation
4 Pay
5 Satisfaction

Margaret, a social services manager
1 Appreciation
2 Satisfaction
3 Status and position
4 Recognition
5 Pay

These examples show that the mix of performance reward elements can and will vary from person to person. The individual desires and needs that people have are reflected in the way that they look at performance reward systems. The best systems are those which recognize this variety and don't try to force a particular ranking on everyone. Of course designing performance reward systems which cater for and reflect individual needs calls for considerable creativity. How this can be done successfully is explored further in Chapter 15.

Motivation

Does performance reward motivate people to perform better? It is an important question.

Experience over the last fifty years with various forms of pay systems has shown that money does not, on its own, motivate higher levels of performance. It appears that meeting Maslow's 'higher' level needs is more likely to engender improved performance. In other words people have to want to perform better for themselves first and foremost. Without the desire to want to do it the old 'carrot and the stick' philosophy will just not suffice.

If the 'human TOUCH' is missing no amount of coercion or financial persuasion will work. Roger Harrison puts it this way in his book *The Collected Papers of Roger Harrison*:[6]

- Give credit for people's ideas and build on their contributions.
- Listen to people's concerns, hopes, fears, pain: be there for them when they need an empathetic ear.
- Treat people's feelings as important.
- Be generous with your trust. Give others the benefit of the doubt.
- See others as valuable and unique in themselves and not simply for their contribution to the task.
- Respond actively to others' needs and concerns; give help and assistance when it is not your job.
- Look for the good and positive in others, and acknowledge it when you find it.
- Nurture others' growth: teach, support, encourage, smooth the path.
- Take care of the organisation. Be responsive and responsible to its needs as a living system.

In this way, Harrison argues, the degree of personal satisfaction, growth and commitment for managers and those they manage will increase considerably and performance with it.

The concept of personal motivation

Some years ago, whilst working with a group of managers, I devised a simple way in which they could get in touch with their own personal motivation. I first described this approach in my book, *The Business of Training*,[7] from which the following is an extract. I defined motivation as:

> The inner force that makes each person pursue courses of action, both positive and negative, which lead to the satisfaction of some desire.

To aspire to our personal fulfilment it is important to have a clear grasp of what will help and hinder us. In addition it helps if we understand our boundaries, both those we set ourselves, and the ones imposed upon us by other people. Finally we need to know how to find the space to breathe and grow.

These four elements of personal motivation impact on each other and it helps to look at all four so that we gain a full picture of how we can motivate ourselves and reach for our potential. The framework in Table 13.1 helps you to do this.

Building blocks

Many of us do not welcome the prospect of making a careful assessment of

Table 13.1   The elements of personal motivation

Building blocks	Barriers
No one can go back and change the past. Whatever has happened to make people who they are has already taken place. People must discover their real strengths and skills. These are the building blocks of their future development.	People allow many things to get in their way. Most of these barriers are self-created, based on messages about ourselves. We need to identify all our barriers and systematically tear them down.
Boundaries	**Breathing space**
We all operate within self-imposed boundaries. We have developed these to help us to survive. If we can see where these are we can start to stretch them as far as we can.	We all need time and space to review where we are. This space is important to refresh and renew ourselves, so plan for it.

ourselves, but we need to do so before we can move on. I am not suggesting a SWOT analysis in the conventional sense because the focus on weaknesses and threats does not provide a good basis for looking at our portfolio of skills and experience. The approach should be to look at two key areas: the development of skills, and the application of those skills. This schedule of learning and experience is your foundation for further growth.

Barriers

There are a great many things that we allow to get in our way. Most of these barriers are self-created. They are the result of many years of conditioning about what we can and cannot do. If someone tells us often enough that we are useless, we come to believe it, just as we tend to believe it if someone tells us how good we are. However, we are usually more ready to believe the bad things about ourselves than the good things.

Identifying our barriers is not easy. We have to take a long hard look at ourselves and be very honest about the things that we know get in the way. When we have produced a list of these we can start to work on dismantling them. Being aware of our barriers is sometimes enough to start the process of removal.

Boundaries

Just as we have been conditioned to accept barriers to our personal achievement, so we have been conditioned to accept boundaries to our growth. The following statements:

- Don't forget your working-class background.
- You're not intelligent enough to get a degree.
- No one in our family has ever done manual work.

all conspire to establish boundaries to our lives.

We need to establish the boundaries that surround us now; then we can start to stretch them further and further until finally we have no limits to our growth.

Breathing space

Personal motivation, to be effective, has to become a regular part of everyday activities. From time to time we will want to review the four key steps. Many things will change and, it is hoped, will keep changing for the better. We should make space for ourselves to think, to learn and to grow.

The space can be alone, or with someone else; indoors, or outdoors; or wherever we feel comfortable and relaxed. Once we have created the space, when and where we want it, we can use it to assess and re-assess where we are, and where we want to be. When we are satisfied that we have breathed in sufficient freshness, we can return.

After looking closely at yourself in this way it is helpful to prepare a statement of your 'personal performance drivers' – the things that you want that will motivate you to perform at your very best. Unless you are clear about your 'performance drivers' how can you expect anyone else to know? Part of this exercise might be to look at the five elements of performance reward and list them in the order that are important to you. This helps you to specify the reward system that would best suit your needs.

Organizations often design reward systems based on massive and incorrect assumptions about what their people want. This, and not taking account of individual 'performance drivers', serves only to create reward systems which do not motivate people. The key to motivation is to ask what people want and to listen to what they say.

Pressing the 'GO' button

In this context 'GO' stands for 'Greatness and Opportunity'. When all the performance factors are right and when individuals are motivated by their inner desire for self-fulfilment and satisfaction, then greatness is possible. Creating opportunities for people to excel themselves is the primary role of all managers. Pressing the 'GO' button is a rare occurrence for most managers and performers.

So much has to be in tune with the people, the organization culture, the times, the circumstances, that it seems hardly possible for the 'GO' button to ever get pressed.

Performance reward is one of the many triggers that can possibly make it happen if, and only if, the elements of performance reward are in exactly the right mix and volume for the person concerned. This matching of performance reward to individual preference is rare except at the higher levels of organizations. But then perhaps 'greatness' is reserved for the chosen few at the top. Yet as Peters and Waterman[8] discovered, organizations perform excellently when 'ordinary people perform extraordinarily'.

The key then to high performance could be to persuade people at all levels that greatness is possible and to train managers to seek out and press their 'GO' buttons. There is no better way to bridge the performance gap than to provide exactly what people need to perform and to reward them in tune with their own preference.

References

1 Maslow, A.H., *Motivation and Personality*, Harper and Row, New York, 1954.
2 Herzberg, F., Mausner, B. and Snyderman, B.B., *The Motivation to Work*, John Wiley and Sons Inc., New York, 1959.
3 Peters, T.J., and Waterman, R.H., *In Search of Excellence – Lessons from America's Best run Companies*, Harper and Row, New York, 1982.
4 Blanchard, K., and Johnson, S., *The One Minute Manager*, Collins, London, 1983.
5 Peter, L.J., *The Peter Principle*, Souvenir Press, London, 1994.
6 Harrison, Roger, *The Collected Papers of Roger Harrison*, McGraw-Hill, London, 1995.
7 Bentley, Trevor J., *The Business of Training*, McGraw-Hill, London, 1990.
8 Peters and Waterman, op. cit.

14   Financial rewards

This chapter deals with issues of designing flexible pay systems that reward people in an individual and specific way appropriate to their preference and the circumstances of their work.

Financial performance drivers

In modern society, where everything is valued in financial terms and where money is the means and power of exchange, people have to have money. It is necessary.

The first important factor of money is the ability of those who have it to satisfy their survival ('lower' level) needs. When this happens people feel secure. Of course needs are different and relative to the society in which we live, but a sense of security is the first step in satisfying our needs.

The next step is to have sufficient money to do the things we want to do and to have the things we want to have. Again what we want to do and have varies for each of us. It depends on many factors from our dependants to our perceived 'essential' lifestyle. One of my friends has paid for all his children to attend private schools. This was, to him, a basic essential of his life. In the 1950s in the UK only the 'very well off' had telephones, motor cars and television. In the 1990s all of these are taken for granted as basic necessities.

The idea of having 'enough' has never taken root. Politically it cannot be allowed to take root. Politicians and industrialists maintain that we must have growth, and this means increased money in circulation and increased consumption. The idea is that our standard of living rises as we have more money so that we can spend more. This philosophy plays down, or ignores, the values of clean air, abundant water, open roads, open countryside, unpolluted beaches, peace and quiet and time to enjoy it, and all the other elements of a quality life. But, like it or not, most people are hooked into the system, and it is one that is very hard to break out of.

It is no surprise, therefore, to discover that financial rewards are a significant performance driver, not in the sense of achieving the highest levels of performance, but at least enough to keep the job that provides the money we need. When additional financial rewards are on offer there is some motivation for some people to do more, but it is usually only the minimum extra effort to get the extra money. There are of course exceptions to this, where people will perform at exceptional levels to achieve very high financial rewards even when they don't need the money.

Lotteries are a very good way of examining attitudes to money. Millions of people are willing to spend a small amount of money and effort in order to win enough never to have to perform, in terms of work, again.

What are we paid for?

We can gain a much clearer picture of how financial reward operates if we look at it in terms of what people are paid for. This breaks down into three elements (as depicted in Table 14.1):

● what we bring
● what we do
● what we produce.

What we bring

Many pay systems work on the basis of what people bring to the work, perhaps the most common being the time and effort they spend on the job. Pay by the hour, the day, the week and the month is common practice, and

Table 14.1   The elements of financial reward

What we bring	What we do	What we produce
INPUT	JOB	OUTPUT
Time	Position	Items produced
Skills	Responsibility	Output delivered
Talent	Authority	Business created

overtime is a well known element of much manual and semi-skilled work. Time was such an important factor that for many years most working people had to 'clock on and off' to prove how long they had been at work. Being late and/or absent was punished by a reduced pay packet.

This emphasis on time has slowly changed as more of the work that people do has become skilled. Today it is more likely that people will receive a wage or salary that is agreed on a regular basis rather than a weekly wage packet based on the hours worked, though of course this practice still continues.

A regular salary is paid on the expectation that people bring a range of required skills to their work. The application of these skills may still take place within a structured time frame, but the hours aren't counted. The result is that people often work longer hours for the same pay, i.e. overtime does not operate. As the need for skills increases people can expect to be paid larger salaries, even if they continue to do the same job. The person is more skilled and experienced and is paid more for the same work.

The third thing people bring to their work is talent. Musicians, designers, architects, artists, writers, actors, sportsmen and women, and so on, are paid for their particular abilities. This is sometimes in the form of a regular salary, but more often than not it is in the form of a fee for a particular service. The more rare and/or special the talent the higher the fees.

So our work is valued and rewarded on the basis that whatever we bring creates value that is at least equivalent to what we are paid. In reality for an organization to pay us in the first place it has to believe that we will produce, or contribute to the production of, value beyond what we cost, so that the organization can pay its overheads and make a profit. This 'added value' phenomenon has contributed to a great deal of dispute between employees and employers over the years.

What we do

The second element changes the focus from 'what we bring' to 'what we do', but of course to do our job means that we bring with us, or it is assumed that we bring with us, the ability needed to do it. The reason for this change of focus is necessary because people are promoted not because of an increase in their skills or talent, but because they are prepared to take on a 'position' that may have greater levels of 'responsibility' and more 'authority'. Promotion also has a lot to do with other factors such as political skills, age, length of service and 'who you know'. Often promotion also means that the link between pay and performance becomes ever more tenuous because people are paid more whether or not their contribution increases.

Taking on a position means taking on the risk of standing out from the other people in the workplace. This separation and isolation can bring with it increased stress and this should be reflected in the financial rewards that are offered. There are countless examples of skilled workers who have taken on the positions of chargehands and supervisors and have found the extra pay did not recompense them for the loss of friendship and belonging.

A new position usually, but not always, brings the added burden of responsibility. Being responsible for something other than your own skills and your own work, i.e. being responsible for the work of others, is an onerous task. It is often taken on too lightly by people who have no idea what it means and who make a bad job of it. People should not be given or asked to take on responsibilities that they are not ready for, but many are. The reward of a higher salary again does not compensate for feeling inadequate, worrying and not enjoying work.

Authority is one element that is jealously guarded by those high up in organizations. Although they like to delegate responsibility they are often loathe to delegate authority. As the majority of managers will know, in reality this should be the other way round. Management should delegate authority wherever possible and retain responsibility for the outcomes. Authority is often even seen as a reward in itself. 'You now have the authority to …' is handed out like a bonus. Authority and its proper use should be highly rewarded, but often it is overlooked and lost in the mixture of position and responsibility.

What we produce

Counting the items produced (piecework) has been used for many years as a way of relating pay to performance and for creating the incentive to increase productivity. It has had some notable successes and even more notable failures. It is in essence a very direct way of linking pay to work, but only where the influence of people on output is the dominant factor. With mechanisation and automation piecework has had a limited life, and yet can still be found in operation today.

Paying people for what they 'deliver' (in the sense of make happen or produce) is becoming more popular as a significant amount of specialist work is 'contracted out' to skilled artisans. It is likely that much more attention will be given in the future to how people can be rewarded for what they deliver.

Selling or creating business opportunities is the one area of performance where pay is closely linked to the volume of business generated. This is usually done via some direct commission as a percentage of the business generated. It is an aspect of performance-related pay that is most often used as an example why PRP cannot operate in non-selling working situations. 'Oh, you can do that with selling, but not with my job' is an oft heard comment.

All the aspects of being paid for 'what we produce' clearly relate pay to the 'output' measures of performance and so lend themselves to being considered as the prime focus for PRP. However, there is a significant problem. If we use this particular focus we also have to ensure that the product is of the right quality, and is produced in the right way.

How money corrupts

There is always a possibility that people might use their position and/or influence to obtain money that has nothing to do with their performance or their work, for example in the giving of favours such as meals, accommodation, air fares and so on. The problem lies not with the use of money as a means of reward, but with the constant pressure to have more which seems to affect some people. This push to 'keep up with the Jones's' or to 'improve one's lot' can present a constant temptation to cross the line between the reasonable and unreasonable use of position and power. It is one of the dangers of placing too much or too large an emphasis on money as a means of performance reward.

Putting financial rewards in their place

Financial rewards serve four basic purposes in the overall package of performance reward:

- to satisfy 'lower' level needs
- to provide a measure of personal value or worth
- to provide a basis for comparison with others
- to act, for some people, as a performance driver.

Basic needs

The first and most important purpose of financial reward is to meet the basic needs of people for which they provide their skills, etc. Some form of financial reward has to be paid. Of course there are situations, such as charity and community work, where people will bring their skills for nothing, but they can only do this if their basic needs are being met in some other way.

A measure of personal worth

Some people seem to value themselves in terms of their earning power. This is perfectly understandable when society values people in this way. The more they earn the more their self-esteem increases, and it can have an overpowering effect on their attitude to paid work. When I am counselling senior managers who have been made redundant perhaps the worst aspect of losing their high paid jobs is the complete removal of their personal value system. With the job goes all their confidence, self-esteem and reason for existing. This is particularly true of 'workaholics', some of whom become suicidal.

A basis of comparison

One of the first questions people ask, or want to ask, when they meet someone for the first time is, 'What do you do?' The answer allows them to place the person in a status list or 'pecking order'. They can compare themselves and decide where they relate in this list to the other person. This process of comparison becomes quite addictive and can be seen in the way the consumer market is divided demographically into A, B, C (the top people) and D, E, F (the bottom people) according to their spending power. We read about society being divided into the 'haves' and the 'have nots'. Whether we like it or not financial reward is a comparative measure that people and society will use.

A performance driver

Financial reward acts for some people as a performance driver, providing the prod they need to work harder and perform better. This is usually only true for those who have the attitude of doing the minimum to earn their pay. For people who already do their best for what they are paid, being offered more is virtually an insult. *People Management* (24 August 1995) reported that John Hoddinott, the chief constable of Hampshire, turned down an appointment that had an element of PRP saying: 'The notion that I will work harder or more effectively because of performance related pay is absurd and objectionable, if not insulting.'

Pay according to need

The anthroposophic movement which follows the ideas of Rudolf Steiner, the Austrian philosopher, uses the concept of paying people what they need rather than the 'pay for what you do' system. This means that a single person doing a particular job may be paid less than a married person with dependent children. The question when people come to work with anthroposophic organizations is not 'Will you accept this pay package?' but 'What do you need to come and work with us?'

This approach works best in organizations that operate as communities with shared responsibilities and involvement of everyone in the decision-making processes. In some cases there are central funds, or kitties, that can be used by individuals for special needs in agreement with the community.

The first reaction of most organizations to this approach is 'It couldn't work here'. Perhaps this is true, because it requires a selfless attitude and an acceptance that others have greater and lesser needs than we do. However, there is a place for some element of reward according to need. A pay system should include some measure of 'needs test' for people to do the work effectively.

Designing financial reward systems

Few organizations take the trouble to design and build creative and innovative financial reward systems that cope effectively with individual and organizational needs. Many pay systems operate within tightly constrained job grading structures that allow little flexibility and which place too great an emphasis on the 'what we bring', and 'what we do' elements of reward. People increase their financial reward in these systems mainly by moving up the grading structure, or by receiving increments within a particular band for length of service or skills acquired.

To see how divisive these systems can be you only have to work in an organization that operates them and to hear people described as, 'She's a grade 4, and I need a grade 5 for this job' or 'I work hard to give my grade 4s a chance to participate in the planning process'.

In less structured systems, but where a hierarchy exists, pay levels and salary amounts are kept secret. People are not encouraged to talk about what they earn. Perhaps there is something to hide. Perhaps equality and fairness of treatment are missing. Perhaps the comparative nature of financial rewards will create some disagreement and disruption.

There is no 'perfect' financial reward system. It is possible to design and implement good flexible systems that pay attention to five important factors. The first two factors determine the way the financial reward package is constructed and managed. The next three factors determine the size and shape of the package. The factors are:

- the personal preferences of people
- the needs of individuals

- the nature of the work
- taking account of what we are paid for
- how people perform.

Personal preferences

In the modern high technology world it is possible to create and operate systems which present an extensive range of options for pay packages that meet people's personal preferences. These should cater for choices about when we are paid, how much in money and how much in other forms such as rent, cars, loans, pensions, savings and so on. The pay package can be constructed in an amazing variety of ways to suit virtually any personal preference.

Personal needs

Individuals may have financial needs such as monthly mortgage repayments that they want the company to pay direct for them. They might want their child care, or credit card loans to be paid off. Others might want their money paid into a current account for living expenses and a savings account for monthly and quarterly bills. Some might want personal financial and/or tax advice. There is so much that could be done to help people cope with their personal financial needs, and yet it rarely is.

The nature of the work

The nature of the work that people do varies considerably in terms of the demands that it makes on them. Some work in a quiet, reflective environment where there is a considerable amount of concentration and creative thought. Others may work in a hectic environment, dealing with queues of people who all seem to be in a hurry. The range of possibilities is enormous. Pay packages should take account of the nature of the work and include appropriate weightings on the rate of pay.

What we are paid for

Financial reward packages should identify separately the amounts we are paid for the three elements of 'what we bring', 'what we do' and 'what we produce'. The proportion that falls into each category will, of course, vary depending on the job and the nature of the work.

For example, salespeople may have a package divided as follows:

- what they bring   £500 per month
- what they do   £200 per month
- what they produce   £1000–£4000 per month

and chartered management accountants may have a package that looks like this:

- what they bring   £1500 per month
- what they do   £1000 per month
- what they produce   £1000–£1500 per month

Financial reward that pays attention to these three aspects of the working contract is very effective. People can see how they can improve their pay by increasing skills, by taking on more responsibility and authority and from how they perform. In the example of salespeople there may be very little financial advantage from taking on additional responsibility, say for managing a sales team, compared to increasing sales volume.

A good financial reward system shows people how they can benefit from different forms of personal development. Promotion to a higher position should not be the only way to earn more from doing more.

Paying for performance

When we talk about paying for performance we should be talking about personalized individual performance and team performance. Large company schemes that give a share in profit or some overall performance bonus are not effective performance reward approaches. They are too distant from the work of the individual and too easily manipulated by the organization.

Pay for performance should be one element of the pay package and paid as a reward for what we produce exactly in line with our agreed performance plan, and the amount known at the time the plan is agreed. It is important that people know for certain what their performance related pay will be if they achieve the agreed planned level of output.

This then becomes a real motivation to perform. To work towards achieving performance plans and then to have to wait for some declaration by head office of money available for the performance bonus is definitely NOT a way to motivate people or to relate pay and performance. (Chapter 15 explores this further.)

The sensitivity of financial reward

Nothing is more likely to cause problems than pay issues that do not take full account of what people need and want. For some reason there is a reticence and a difficulty in dealing with matters concerning financial rewards. It seems that there is still a gulf between employers and employees regarding pay. Why issues of pay are not always dealt with out in the open and in a participative way defies understanding.

Senior managers sometimes seem to forget that they are seen as role models by people both within and outside the organisation. So that when they award themselves large pay increases and then preach pay restraint, it is no surprise that this appears incongruent and insensitive. This closed mind attitude and short sightedness bedevils the subject of financial reward. If the organization's pay and reward system is patently unfair, then it will do more to damage employees' commitment, productivity and morale than almost anything top managers might say or do.

It could be so different if everyone in the organization were to be part of the same flexible financial reward system with the same choices and options.

15 Linking pay and performance

Few subjects give rise to more heated debate than that of linking pay and performance. When employers suggest it the immediate reaction of employees and their representatives is: 'They want to pay less money for more output'. And when employees and their representatives suggest it, it is because: 'They want more money for less output'. What a sorry state of affairs it is when people can't sit down together and arrive at an appropriate and meaningful way of linking pay and performance so that everyone can benefit. Surely this is what everyone wants?

The links between performance and pay

There are some situations where the link between performance and pay is very clear and very direct. Many years ago I spent a few months working as a commission only financial adviser. My pay was linked directly to my performance and I knew as I was selling a particular product what my pay would be. The pressure was to sell as much as I could and to work as hard as I could to make a good living. I enjoyed the income I generated, but the pressure was so intense that I returned to working as a financial director. The pay was not as good, but in comparison the job was easy and almost pressure free.

For golf professionals who play on tour the link between performance and pay is similarly direct and known at the time the performance is, or is not, taking place. Even the most successful golfers have to keep winning to retain their lucrative sponsorship deals.

The skilled carpenter who works alone has to obtain work and produce good quality results in order to be paid and to continue to obtain work on the basis of reputation for quality and reliability. The link here between performance and pay is clear and quite direct.

163

However, for the vast majority of people working as employees for organizations pay has only a rather tenuous link to their performance. It is in this particular context where so many problems arise.

Some links that don't work

Profit sharing is NOT performance-related pay. It is too remote from the individual to have a clear and calculated link with what the person actually does. Profit sharing, whether in payment of money or issuing shares, does give employees a sense of 'having a stake' in the business and is valuable from this point of view, but it has nothing to do with individual performance.

Bonuses paid for 'doing well' are only vaguely related to performance. Most bonus systems are at the subjective whim of management and also fail to have a direct link, unless they are calculated in accordance to some measured standard of performance which is directly related to an individual's output.

Schemes that link some additional payment to the subjective appraisal ratings that are assessed once a year, also do not work. In fact such schemes are widely mistrusted because they are usually manipulated by management according to some predefined standard distribution of ratings, which is partly to control the level of payouts and partly to 'keep people in their places'.

Systems that provide a lump sum out of profits, which is distributed locally by business units in relation to the contribution they made to profits, are again too remote and too easily manipulated for staff to have confidence in receiving a payout that directly reflects their hard work. The focus becomes 'keeping the boss sweet' rather than performance.

The reasons why many individual PRP schemes have failed is evident:

- reward is too remote from performance
- decisions on reward are too subjective
- rewards are manipulated by management
- employees cannot calculate their rewards
- rewards are paid too long after the event
- managements desire 'quick fix' solutions.

Forging links that work

There is no easy way to forge links that work. To do it successfully means finding ways whereby as people perform they can calculate exactly what they will be paid for their performance. And where the reward for the performance is given immediately after the performance takes place, i.e. the next pay day if the reward is financial.

The first stage in forging a successful link is to define what is expected of employees and to indicate what they will be paid if these expectations are met. Chapter 14 looked at how a financial reward package could be constructed from the three factors of 'what we bring', 'what we do' and 'what we produce'. If we use these three factors as a basis for defining what is expected of the individual, then we can relate pay to each of the factors and create a direct link between performance (achieving expectations) and pay.

Go back to the performance planning stage of the performance management cycle (Chapter 8) and look at the process of planning what is expected. The focus in Chapter 8 is on outputs, i.e. 'what we produce', but we also have to consider paying for 'what we bring' and 'what we do', particularly the responsibilities that we take on.

For each of these three aspects of performance it is necessary to decide on a sum of money that will be paid. This will probably be a fixed salary for 'what we bring' and 'what we do', but will vary for 'what we produce' based on the level achieved. If this approach is followed it is quite clear to individuals what they will be paid for each aspect of performance. Performance-related pay can then be paid when the performance is achieved. By doing the work in advance in this way the costs and benefits to the organization of high performance can be calculated and built into the budgets for the forthcoming period.

Performance-related pay

When pay is directly related to performance it is, or should be, also related to the value generated by the desired level of performance. It would, for example, be silly to pay salespeople more commission than the profit generated by the business they bring in. So in order to arrive at a figure of what should be paid for the performance we need to first determine the figure of the value that the performance generates.

Attaching value to results

Attaching value to 'what we bring' and 'what we do' is very difficult and it might be desirable to use some sort of job evaluation process to value these two aspects, particularly when considering the extent of the individual's authority and responsibility. There are a number of well established schemes for job evaluation which can be used for this purpose.

However, it should be possible to arrive at a value for 'what we produce'. This presupposes that the concept of focusing on outputs is being followed. Chapter 8 suggested that for each outcome produced by the individual it was necessary to state what the expected results would be. When we know the expected results it should be possible to place a value on them. Table 15.1 shows an example for a delivery driver.

Table 15.1 Attaching value to results

Outcomes	Results	Values
Goods delivered to customers (80–100pw)	80–100 satisfied customers per week	£400–£500*
Minimum time taken	Reduced cost per delivery	£80–£100+
Shortest route taken	Reduced operating costs	£25‡
Despatches collected	Extra business 20–40 per week	£100–£200§

The figures have been arrived at by looking at the benefits to the business of the results achieved by the driver. These have been calculated as follows:

* Average profit £5 per delivery x deliveries.
+ Average cost per delivery £10 reduced by, say, £1 x no. of deliveries.
‡ Average cost per route £150 reduced by, say, £5 x five routes a week.
§ Average profit £5 per delivery x no. of despatches collected.

Once these performance values have been calculated we can decide the amount of performance-related pay (see Table 15.2). In our example it might be decided that the delivery driver will receive 50 per cent of the cost savings and 10 per cent of the profit earned.

In this example the delivery driver would be paid a standard wage for the

Table 15.2 Calculating performance-related pay

Results	Values	Performance-related pay
80–100 satisfied customers per week	£400–£500	£40–£50
Reduced cost per delivery	£80–£100	£40–£50
Reduced operating costs	£25	£12.50
Extra business 20–40 per week	£100–£200	£10–£20

'what we bring' and 'what we do' aspects of performance. The PRP is for the 'what we produce' aspect of performance. The link is clear, direct and paid weekly or monthly in accordance with performance levels, and can be calculated by the driver.

The employee's formula

The employee's formula is seen as:

> performance-related pay = a proportion of the value generated by performance levels achieved

Because this is clear, direct and can be calculated by people as they are performing, it can have an immediate motivational impact on the work they do. They will also need to pay attention to the five performance factors of: environment, conditions, personal desire, personal state, and personal competence, to ensure that nothing interferes with them performing to their best.

The organization's formula

From the organization's point of view the formula is seen as:

a fair (affordable) proportion of value generated = performance-related pay

By valuing results of performance in this way the organization can see that they can afford to pay the money earned as PRP because the value generated more than covers the cost of paying it. There is no need to wait and see what profits are made by the company. The individual contribution of employees is clear.

Implementing performance-related pay (PRP)

There are five steps in setting up a successful PRP system:

1 Create 'Job profiles' which show what is expected for:
   - 'what we bring'
   - 'what we do'
   - 'what we produce'.
2 Evaluate the pay levels for:
   - 'what we bring'
   - 'what we do'.

3   Calculate 'values generated' for:
   ● 'what we produce'.
4   Decide the proportion of 'value generated' to be shared with performers.
5   Determine the 'financial reward package' that equates with the total pay
    agreed and which reflects individual preference and need.

This may seem an awesome exercise to carry out in terms of time and effort. However, it can be achieved relatively quickly and efficiently by involving everyone in the process. Every performer, from the front-line workers to the boardroom, completes their own 'PRP preparation worksheet' which is reviewed by their immediate manager and then by the PRP implementation group.

In this way not only is the work shared, everyone also feels involved in the whole process. The level of involvement is very important in developing and implementing PRP.

The timing of performance-related pay

The first golden rule for successful PRP is:

> Payment for performance should be made as close as possible to the moment of achievement.

The world moves on very fast and waiting to be paid for achievements that happened in the past keeps performers focused backwards instead of on the next performance 'stagepost'. It is almost impossible to build performance bridges while looking backwards.

If we want to bridge the performance gap we have to pay for each step forward *as it happens*.

Annual performance-related pay systems do not work because the time gap is too great for people to make the link between their performance and what they receive in terms of bonus. Some organizations are of the opinion 'that until the values generated by individual performance work their way through to the bottom line we don't know how much we can afford to pay'. The answer is simple, work it out monthly, or weekly. The technology exists to do it.

Individual and team performance

The second golden rule for successful PRP is:

Performance should be measured and rewarded at the individual and, in some cases, team level.

To move any higher than this waters down the link between people's performance and their contribution and reward. If a divisional and/or company bonus is paid *in addition* to the individual performance reward, then it has the value of linking the individual's performance with that of the organization as a whole.

In the case where a job is done by a team, i.e. it cannot be done by an individual because the output of the activity can only be produced by a team, then all that has been said about 'job profiles' and 'values generated' etc. would apply to the team as if it were an individual. Performance pay is made to the team and they can then decide on individual contributions according to some agreed basis and share the team reward accordingly.

When inputs come from individuals and outputs come from teams there is a tendency to assess the performance of both with the same criteria. This is not possible. We need to look at the outputs of individuals as inputs to the team and then assess the team output separately (see Figure 15.1).

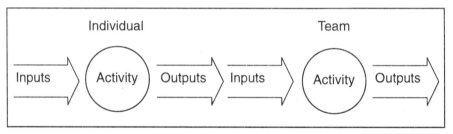

Figure 15.1   Individual and team performance

The individual outputs will be used for assessing individual performance and the team outputs for assessing team performance. This approach helps to clarify what is expected from each member of the team and to define responsibilities accordingly. It is much easier than it might at first seem and is a method which links well into a performance management system based on assessing individual performance.

Team PRP should not be used where individual PRP is hard to implement. It should only be used where there is a very close and unarguable link between the cooperative efforts of a group of people which results in a measurable output. To work successfully team-based PRP needs the following:

● clearly defined team output
● a clear link between individual efforts and the team's achievement

- cooperative and supportive conditions and working environment
- well established team relationships.

Successful PRP ultimately depends upon designing a system which fits closely with reality and fully reflects the way people work and produce performance outputs.

16   Recognition

I exist. I matter. People know I am here. I want to be acknowledged. When I perform I want to be noticed and I want to be appreciated for what I do.

> The greatest humiliation in life, is to work hard on something from which you expect great appreciation, and then get none.
>
> Edgar Watson Howe[1]

We are all human and have the same basic needs to be seen and appreciated for who we are and what we contribute. Many organizations take the attitude that it is not appropriate to appreciate and praise people. There is a hardness and a toughness which seems to remove the more humane aspects of personal relationships. Of course this is a gross generalization and there are other organizations where this attitude does not prevail. However, it is common and one which serves to widen the performance gap rather than to bridge it.

> One good deed dying tongueless
> Slaughters a thousand waiting upon that.
>
> William Shakespeare[2]

The basis of recognition

Recognition, or receiving attention and being favourably noticed, is one of Maslow's 'higher' level needs which he places under the heading of esteem. It has to come before self-actualization, because if we are not noticed by others how can we notice ourselves? Recognition confirms our existence and forms our view of ourselves.

There are five aspects of recognition that have to be present in any successful performance management system:

- being seen
- being valued
- being respected
- being important
- being 'best' at.

Being seen

Being seen is both literal and metaphorical. It is important that people actually 'see' you, that they know you are there. Some people ensure this happens by paying attention to their appearance and dress so that they are 'noticed'. If they stand out then they will be seen. It is interesting that certain organizations deliberately prevent this by having their staff wear uniforms so everyone looks the same. In such situations people have to find other ways of being noticed.

In the metaphorical sense you want your existence and presence to be noticed by and through the way you contribute in your work. Your performance – what you do, how you do it and the outcomes – becomes a picture you paint of who you are. Add this to your physical appearance, i.e. being present, can create a strong sense of who you are. To achieve this you might have to be assertive, make your voice heard, and participate in what is going on. If you hang back and stay in the background you could, metaphorically, disappear.

When managers acknowledge people and notice they are there it reinforces their sense of self. Such acknowledgement can be in very simple ways, from always using people's names when addressing them, to saying thank you for the smallest thing that they do, to formal recognition for some major achievement. Regular, small indications of acknowledgement are often more appreciated than the grand occasions.

Being valued

Being valued follows closely on the heels of being noticed. It happens when some 'appreciation' is added to the acknowledgement. Once again it does not have to be some 'over the top' appreciation or 'gushing' praise. It is often quite sufficient to say something like, 'Thank you, your help has been most useful in us winning the contract' or 'I noticed how you dealt with Mrs Smith and I thought you handled it very skilfully'. In both these examples there is recognition, there is some appreciation and the comments are about specific events.

This last point is very important. Generalized appreciation that cannot be linked to some event that has happened, or is happening, is very hard to believe. People like to hear comments such as 'I like the way you deal with customers it is very effective', but what does it mean and which customers, when? If comments are specific, people can relate them to what happened which often reinforces their own good feelings about what they have done. Imagine that you do something well, you know you have done it well and you will feel pleased with yourself. If your manager appreciates what you did on that specific occasion your own sense of worth is reinforced and enhanced.

Early in our lives we possibly received a great many negative messages about our behaviour and who we were as individuals. This early conditioning may have continued through school so that by the time we come into the world of work we feel unsure and hesitant. If we continue to receive negative affirmations of what we do and who we are, we block our potential. If on the other hand we start to receive acknowledgement and appreciation we are encouraged to explore more of our potential and to grow and develop. And in this way our performance improves.

Being respected

When we are seen, acknowledged and appreciated we start to spread our wings and find that we are treated well and respected by our colleagues. This may be noticed in the way that our opinions are sought, and/or the way that people pay attention when we are speaking, and/or how people seek our help, and/or how we become more involved by management in what is happening.

This sense of respect has a distinct and significant effect on our performance. Firstly our confidence increases and we are more prepared to take risks and try out new ways of doing things, secondly our self-worth grows and we tend to increase our commitment to self-development, and thirdly we start to influence the environment and conditions in which we work so that high performance becomes more achievable.

Being important

By the time we reach the point of being noticed, valued and respected we are probably making an important contribution to what is going on. Strangely our contribution might always have been important, but has never been acknowledged as such.

Scenario – qualifying sales leads

Marion worked for a busy sales department in a large company making electronic equipment for industrial measurement. Her job was to receive written and telephone enquiries and to speak to potential customers to establish what they wanted, whether the company could help and if it seemed worth the effort of a sales representative calling on them. She did this job with great skill and over 75 per cent of the people she asked sales staff to call on became customers.

George, the sales manager, hardly ever used Marion's name when he spoke to her. He did not appreciate her work, or if he did he never mentioned it. She was not involved in sales meetings and the only thanks she received was from the sales staff in the form of, 'Thanks for that great lead you sent me'. Marion described George as polite, businesslike and a little distant.

George retired and the new sales manager, David, invited each of his staff for a meeting to talk about their work. When it was Marion's turn this is what happened.

David　　　　　　　Hello Marion. I've been looking forward to talking to you. All the sales staff are very complimentary about the way you sort out the enquiries and that it saves them a lot of time. I want to know more about how you do it.

Marion sits quietly for a moment, stunned by this unexpected acknowledgement and appreciation.

Marion　　　　　　I'm sorry, but you've taken me by surprise. I had no idea people felt like that.

David　　　　　　　Well they do.

Marion　　　　　　It's going to take me a while to get used to the idea.

Marion then told David how she spoke to the potential customers and the questions she asked and how she had drawn up her own questionnaire which, when she had completed it, enabled her to decide whether to just send some leaflets or arrange a sales visit.

David　　　　　　　I'm impressed. In ten years of being a sales manager I don't think I've come across a better sales qualifying procedure. You've obviously had sales training at some time.

Marion　　　　　　Thank you, but I haven't had any formal sales training. I have just listened to what the sales staff said and developed my own approach.

David　　　　　　　Well I think you have a lot to offer. I want you to attend the sales meeting next week and tell everyone what you do and how they can help you with more regular feedback.

David and Marion began to work closely together. David was always appreciative and suggested Marion should go on a sales training course and regularly attend the sales meeting. Six months later Marion was appointed assistant sales manager.

Being 'best' at

Not all people aspire to being 'best' at anything, but some do and achieving this accolade can, for them, be a significant performance driver. There have been many ideas on how to provide recognition for being 'best':

- photographs seen in some hotels with the heading 'employee of the month'
- regular 'personal profile' of high performers in 'in-house' magazines
- articles in local newspapers about personal achievements
- driving the super sports car for a month for being best salesperson
- awards for being 'best at ...'
- prizes and gifts, including free holidays
- special opportunities for 'executive development courses'
- a week shadowing the chief executive
- a period of work in some exotic overseas location.

These are all ways of 'public' recognition that some people dream about and others shun. They will not appeal to everyone, and thought should be given to how to appeal to those who would shun such public display.

There are many ways in which people can be recognized in a less public way than described above. A personal letter from the chief executive is one way that tells people that their performance has been brought to the boss's attention, that they have been noticed and appreciated at the highest level, and for some this can be a powerful motivation.

Creating systems and procedures for providing recognition is an important part of the overall performance reward package. It is possible to devise highly imaginative and effective ways of focusing attention on performance and people and this kind of focus is exactly what helps to bridge the performance gap.

Building recognition into the performance reward system

Chapter 14 looked at the five crucial factors in constructing a successful reward system, including personal preference and the needs of individuals. These two factors apply equally to the recognition component of reward as they do to the financial component. If people prefer private recognition they will not welcome public recognition. If their need is for regular supportive feedback to maintain confidence, then 'being best' prizes will leave them cold. In other words the approach should be tailored to the people. We are all different and react and respond differently to various stimuli.

Performance x recognition = achievement

It is hard to keep up a strong sense of achievement if the only voice we hear singing our praises is our own. We can, should and do tell ourselves when we do well and it is a pleasant feeling. After a while, when we don't hear any other voices raised in recognition of what we have done, we quite naturally begin to wonder if we have achieved anything at all.

Of course when we set ourselves personal aims and we meet them, then we have definitely achieved something, but add to our own knowing the sound of someone else's knowing and the sense of achievement is enhanced and grows.

Performance without recognition is performance. Performance with recognition is achievement, and the more the recognition the higher the achievement.

Letting individuals know

To receive recognition from others, the others have to know what we have done. Some years ago a tele-sales woman told me that she worked with a group of twenty people in a large room and when they made a sale they hit a bell on their desk and stood up and everyone cheered. This is a particularly direct and immediate system and not everyone would like to work in this way. However, if recognition is to be part of the reward system there has to be a way for people to know about each other's achievement.

Letting the team know

In teamwork the recognition of achievement is usually something that becomes part of the team culture, but there is still a need for the performance to be communicated clearly to everyone in the team. When football players score, their team mates know about it immediately and respond very quickly and the cheers of the crowd are almost deafening. In less focused and less immediate teamwork the 'news' has to be communicated to other team members.

Letting the world know

The broader horizon – the company as a whole and the wider world – has to be part of a comprehensive recognition approach for those people that it suits. In individual and team recognition the performer's feedback is important. It is the sound of others' voices raised in appreciation which is the recognition. In the case of the world the simple fact that the 'news' has been transmitted to the world is recognition in itself and feedback from people who have 'heard the news' is, in a sense, a bonus.

'Performance update'

If we accept that 'blowing one's own trumpet' tends to irritate other people, then other ways have to be found of communicating the information about people's achievements. One way of doing this is to establish a regular method of communicating the 'news' which we can call 'performance update'. This can be in a variety of different forms to cover the three levels of individual, team and world (see Table 16.1).

Table 16.1   Performance update

Method	Individual	Team	World
Internal memo	X	X	
Announcement at departmental/team meetings	X	X	
Circular	X	X	
Notice boards	X	X	
Company magazine	X	X	X
Local network	X	X	X
Internet	N	N	X
Regional business magazines	N	N	X
Trade magazines	N	N	X
Local newspapers	N	N	X
Local radio	N	N	X
Local TV	N	N	X
The national media	N	N	N

In the table X denotes acceptable ways and N indicates ways which are not acceptable for the level shown. It is not a good idea for a close colleague to hear about some achievement of a colleague from, say, the Internet or the local radio. In other words, recognition has to be handled carefully and appropriately for it to have the value of motivation and reward. In addition everyone involved should know how the system is going to work and experience it working successfully before it will be effective.

Incidentally, you will notice that the national media is not acceptable at any level. This is because they're normally only interested in a 'news' worthy angle and can easily distort the message so that the intended recognition becomes 'infamy'.

References

1   Howe, E.W., *Ventures in Common Sense*, 1919.
2   Shakespeare, William, *The Winter's Tale*, Act 1, Scene 2.

17 Freedom and responsibility

Even contented slaves dream of freedom.

Over a hundred years ago Karl Marx, writing about the plight of the working masses, described their lot as 'wage slavery'. The conditions people worked under and the way they were exploited supported this idea of slavery. Today much has changed for the better, but people are still trapped or 'hooked' into a system of 'economic bondage'.

This is, perhaps, the 'shadow' side of financial reward. Whilst pay satisfies the needs of those who earn it, they in turn have, to various degrees, to sacrifice their freedom. Today we still consider full-time employment to mean working eight hours a day, five days a week, 48 weeks a year. And we do this for approximately 40 years before we earn the right to retire. In fact the main attraction of the national lottery is the security and freedom from work and worry that the money would bring.

So what does freedom mean for most of us?

> Perfect freedom is reserved for the man who lives by his own work, and in that work does what he wants to do.
>
> R. G. Collingwood[1]

We cannot have freedom without the responsibility for using it to the advantage of self and others. When we strive at the bidding of others we are not free in the sense of choosing what we do, nor are we responsible for our efforts. People work harder and better when they do it for themselves than they ever will when they do it for others. It is the exercise of choice and desire which signals freedom in the workplace.

Freedom as a reward

Freedom for people to operate more independently in terms of when, how and, sometimes, where they work can be a significant spur to performance. For this to happen they need to display their willingness and ability to take full responsibility for producing the outputs that are expected from them.

The question of boundaries

Such freedom that people earn in their work falls within certain boundaries, beyond which they will only operate with the agreement of colleagues and management. As trust grows and the capacity for responsibility increases, the boundaries can be extended.

In this context boundaries are seen less as limits, more as 'territory' demarcations. They indicate where one person's responsibility ends and another's starts. This is very important in ensuring good relationships. People learn to respect others' boundaries and in return have their boundaries respected. In this way freedom can flourish within personal 'territories'.

Freedom and personal issues

People have a different sense of and need for freedom. To some 'freedom with responsibility' is scary.

> Liberty means responsibility.
> That is why most men dread it.
>
> George Bernard Shaw[2]

People like the idea of freedom, but for many the burden of responsibility is too great so they are prepared to sacrifice their freedom to avoid responsibility. This is a choice that people make, but many do not see it as a choice (which is exercising freedom), but as something which they 'have to do' because of their circumstances. They do, therefore, choose not to be free and then, in some cases, bemoan their lack of freedom.

For others freedom is paramount and they are prepared to accept the responsibility that goes with making choices. For such people freedom is a highly motivating reward.

In between these extremes are a range of attitudes towards freedom which can vary depending upon people's situations. They may not experience freedom at work, nor want to, whilst at home they enjoy their freedom and revel in doing exactly what they want to do.

Of course, if we want to live as 'law abiding' citizens we all experience limits to our freedom which we accept. Those who don't accept the limits imposed by society's laws are marginalized and punished by society. We may also be prepared to limit our freedom in terms of our relationships, where we need to consider the impact of what we do on those close to us. So freedom is a matter of degree and personal choice, and in being able to exercise such choice we are exercising our freedom.

Responsibility as the price of freedom

When we exercise freedom and make choices we also have to take responsibility for the outcomes of the choices that we make.

Personal responsibility

If people choose to take time off they can make arrangements in advance so that their choice is known and the outcomes can be catered for. If they choose to take a day off without any prior notice the outcomes will be considerably different and they will have to accept and deal with the consequences. Making arrangements in advance to take time off is one of the boundaries that people accept to their freedom in order to minimize the impact on others. Being responsible in this way usually means that people have more freedom to take time off.

Responsibility for performance

In the same way if people take full responsibility for their own performance and make arrangements that help them to achieve their expectations, they will usually have the freedom to do so. Paying attention to the five performance factors of environment, conditions, personal desires, personal state and personal competence and doing whatever is possible to improve all of them in a responsible way will lead to both more freedom and improved performance.

The alternative choice is to do little or nothing and to blame others for the inadequacy of the performance factors and to fail to perform. This leads to less freedom and increased pressure and control over how people work. That this approach should ever be chosen indicates that one of two situations prevail:

- either the organization does not offer people the freedom for their own performance, in which case it deserves the inevitable outcome of poor performance, or

- the people themselves choose not to take and use the freedom they are offered, in which case they deserve the inevitable outcome of feeling constrained and controlled by the organization.

Responsibility for others and leadership

Managers are given responsibility for the performance of others. This is part of the manager's job in which often they have had least training and the least ability.

People who have been responsible for their own performance and who have done well are promoted as a reward for their achievement. The promotion often includes being responsible for other people and this is where problems start. Many newly promoted people do not have enough self-confidence as managers to give those they manage the freedom to be responsible for their own performance.

Leadership is about trust and confidence in others, together with the ability to encourage them to trust themselves and to take full responsibility for their own performance. It means giving people the freedom they need to perform.

> The leader's job is to facilitate and illuminate what is happening. Interfere as little as possible. Interference, however brilliant, creates a dependency on the leader. The fewer rules the better. Rules reduce freedom and responsibility.
> Good leadership consists of doing less and being more.
>
> John Heider[3]

Freedom, responsibility and performance

When you are free to pay attention to all the factors which play a part in your performance and free to decide how you are going to perform, then and only then will you be able to do your best. This link between commitment, freedom and personal power is crucial. When you are doing what you are doing because you are choosing to do it to achieve what you want to achieve then you call upon everything you have to perform at your best.

With this commitment and motivation also comes the responsibility for what you produce and for the consequences of your actions. When you meet barriers to your performance, if you have the freedom, you can tackle them creatively and find ways to overcome them or to circumvent them. Without the freedom and responsibility that goes with it, the barriers become reasons that explains your poor performance: 'I couldn't do that because ...'. What you want is to be able to say: 'I did this in spite of ...'.

Freedom, responsibility and performance are inextricably linked. None can exist without the others. In combination they are formidable.

Freedom to negotiate boundaries

This chapter has examined earlier the freedom which is exercised within boundaries or 'personal territories'. It is important that people know about and can respect the boundaries of others. Situations will occur when performance can be significantly enhanced if the boundaries can be moved.

Scenario – making the sale

Jane, a trainee estate agent, has some freedom and responsibility for showing people property and 'talking up' a sale. However, her boundary is reached when it comes to negotiating price.

Jane is on a property with potential clients when they tell her that they are very interested and would like to make a provisional offer. The offer is £10,000 less than the asking price. Jane has recently spoken to the owners who told her that they would accept an offer of £7,500 less than the asking price. Jane says that she will have to talk to the owners. The clients ask if she can give them some idea, because they have several more properties to see and what they are offering is their top price.

Jane comes clean and tells the potential clients that she is not authorized to discuss price, but that she thinks the owners would agree. She suggests that they return to the office and fill in the formal offer documents. The potential clients agree to this.

Back at the office Jane reports to her manager what has happened and says that if he gives her permission she thinks she can complete the sale. The manager agrees and after checking some of their details with the clients she calls the owners and negotiates a sale.

In this scenario Jane took a risk for which she also took responsibility and felt free enough to negotiate a different boundary with her manager. He also felt confident enough to trust her. Subsequently this particular boundary to her freedom was relaxed to negotiating within a certain price range.

Sometimes boundaries become fixed and written into 'job descriptions' in such a way that managers and their staff feel obliged to 'follow them to the letter'. This can be quite frustrating and can lead to a fall off in motivation and commitment and inevitably performance. If people are able to exercise more freedom around their boundaries and take responsibility for re-negotiating them, then performance can increase substantially.

Freedom to bridge the performance gap

There are times when people can see that if they take a particular course of action they will be able to bridge the performance gap. If they have the freedom to take such action, whilst knowing that they will also have to take responsibility for the consequences, then they can act and bridge the performance gap. This might mean temporarily moving their own boundaries and taking risks, for which they will accept responsibility. When such situations arise there are two main types of people who will act: those who have the support of their managers to act in this way; and those who may or may not have support but who have sufficient self-confidence and are highly motivated performers. Both these groups of people will prove to be the high performers.

Conclusion

There are many aspects to consider when 'bridging the performance gap', but the most important are freedom and responsibility. When people are constrained in a network of rules and procedures that seek to emphasize control and containment, then performance will be limited.

Releasing personal power means giving people the freedom to express themselves and to reach for and demonstrate their potential. To do this they have to take responsibility for the freedom they exercise, and this has to be balanced by the boundaries within which they have agreed to operate.

Organizations need both control and high performance. These can be counteracting forces – more control means less performance and vice versa. What we are seeking is the creativity and confidence that freedom brings rather than the conformity and mediocrity of control. The answer is to find the balance of the maximum amount of freedom with the minimum of control. It is a very hard balance to find – and it is possible.

References

1   Collingwood, R.G., *Speculum Mentis*, Prologue, 1889–1943.
2   Shaw, G.B., *Maxims for Revolutionists: Liberty*.
3   Heider, J., *The Tao of Leadership*, Wildwood House, Aldershot, 1986.

Index

The Motivation Manual

Gisela Hagemann

Improved productivity, flexible work practices, low rates of absenteeism, commitment to quality, ever-higher standards of customer service - these are the benefits of a well-motivated workforce. In this prize-winning book the author takes modern motivational theory and shows how any manager can apply it to create shared vision, develop mutual trust and involve employees in the decision-making process.

The text is enlivened throughout by examples with which managers will identify and there is a unique final section containing twenty seven exercises designed to strengthen interpersonal skills and improve creativity.

Gower

The Practice of Empowerment

Making the Most of Human Competence

Dennis C Kinlaw

Organizations are downsizing, re-engineering and restructuring at an ever-increasing rate. The challenge now is to find better and better ways of harnessing the mental resources of the people who remain.

Dr Kinlaw, one of America's leading authorities on management development, sees empowerment as a way of improving organizational performance by making the most competent people the most influential most of the time, and his book provides a comprehensive and detailed model for achieving this objective. Drawing on examples and case studies from successful companies, Dr Kinlaw describes a practical, step-by-step process for introducing or extending empowerment in an organization or any part of an organization, and shows how to use feedback, team development and learning to good effect.

For managers considering, or involved in, empowerment programmes, and for concerned HR and training professionals, this new book represents an important resource for improving organizational performance.

Gower

The Techniques of Instruction

Roger James

What do effective instructors do that makes them effective? In this ground-breaking book, Dr James examines the whole process of instruction from the point of view of skill development to discover which are the best techniques and why. He shows:

- how to produce the best trainee performance possible in the shortest possible time
- how to structure practice sessions to maximize learning
- how to analyse the task involved so as to design the most appropriate exercise
- how to deal with the "slow" trainee
- how to boost the trainee's confidence
- how to instruct "at a distance".

Although based on extensive research, the material in the book is presented in non-technical language and draws on a wide range of examples. The result is a comprehensive guide to the practice of instruction which will be of immense value to anyone involved in training, teaching or coaching.

Gower